STEAM

Concepts for Infants and Toddlers

STEAM

CONCEPTS FOR INFANTS AND TODDLERS

Nichole A. Baumgart

Linda R. Kroll

Redleaf Press®
www.redleafpress.org
800-423-8309

Published by Redleaf Press
10 Yorkton Court
St. Paul, MN 55117
www.redleafpress.org

First edition 2018
Cover design by Louise OFarrell
Cover illustrations by iStock/syntika and iStock/A-Digit
Interior design by Louise OFarrell
Typeset in Adobe Arno Pro
Interior photos by Sergei Miadzvezhanka
Printed in the United States of America
25 24 23 22 21 20 19 18   1 2 3 4 5 6 7 8

Library of Congress Cataloging-in-Publication Data
Names: Baumgart, Nichole A., author. | Kroll, Linda Ruth, author.
Title: STEAM concepts for infants and toddlers / Nichole A. Baumgart, Linda
  R. Kroll.
Description: First edition. | St. Paul, MN : Redleaf Press, 2018. | Includes
  bibliographical references.
Identifiers: LCCN 2017058285 (print) | LCCN 2018013495 (ebook) | ISBN
  9781605545554 (ebook) | ISBN 9781605545547 (pbk. : alk. paper)
Subjects: LCSH: Science—Study and teaching (Early childhood) | Arts—Study
  and teaching (Early childhood)
Classification: LCC LB1139.5.S35 (ebook) | LCC LB1139.5.S35 B39 2018 (print)
  | DDC 372.35/044—dc23
LC record available at https://lccn.loc.gov/2017058285

Printed on acid-free paper

This book is dedicated to all the infants, toddlers, teachers, and parents who experimented with STEAM curriculum and helped us learn how best we could learn together. It is also dedicated to all infants and toddlers, who are brilliant problem posers and problem solvers.

Contents

Foreword

STEAM Concepts for Infants and Toddlers by Nichole A. Baumgart and Linda R. Kroll will deepen your appreciation of science, technology, engineering, arts and design, and mathematics in the everyday life of infants and toddlers. Baumgart and Kroll show how STEAM concepts are always in the background of early learning, and the authors provide invaluable guidance on how teachers can bring those concepts into the foreground while respecting infants' and toddlers' self-initiated learning.

This timely book places infants and toddlers at the center of learning and invites teachers to connect with how children make sense of the world around them. Three questions orient the reader:

1. How do we make visible children's STEAM learning and concept development?

2. How do educators facilitate, reflect, and respond to children's work in STEAM concepts?

3. What environments further support infants' and toddlers' explorations of STEAM concepts?

The first chapter frames these questions within a fundamental understanding of infant and toddler development and learning. Rooted in social interactions with adults and other children, early learning occurs within relationships and routines that give the child a sense of emotional security while providing experiences with people, objects, and concepts. The purpose of infants' and toddlers' exploration is not to find a right answer or build specific knowledge. Rather, Baumgart and Kroll illuminate what children are wondering about and trying to make sense of, how they learn through taking on challenges, and how teachers might provide opportunities for their further exploration.

Chapter 2 highlights how developing language, perceptual and motor skills, cognitive concepts, social relationships, and observational learning come together as children explore the medium of clay. Threaded through this book is the theme that adults first model the use of tools and allow the children to explore the medium separately from the tools. This preliminary experience leads the children to further manipulate the medium with the tools and organize and add complexity to their exploration. Like every chapter, this one provides vivid descriptions of the action and context as children learn STEAM concepts. Before interpreting the learning, the authors allow readers to make their own sense of it. Illustrative photos complement the descriptions and invite readers to wonder about what will happen next in the children's learning. Each chapter ends with questions that spark further observation and exploration in a section titled "Future Possibilities and Reflections."

STEAM learning within the routines and rituals of infant and toddler care is the focus of chapter 3. Baumgart and Kroll make visible how children learn to anticipate sequences of steps in routines. When adults carry out routines in a consistent manner, infants and toddlers learn about cause-and-effect relationships and become increasingly able to predict what will happen next. One example illustrates how adults can embed STEAM concepts within routines such as asking children about the number of songs in a daily singing ritual. Moreover, because steps in routines become familiar to children, adults can introduce new steps or variations, thereby adding complexity to STEAM learning that routines offer.

Chapter 4 explores STEAM concepts through multipurpose materials. It discusses how collecting things is a fundamental aspect of STEAM learning. Infants and toddlers naturally collect objects, fill containers, give things to others, and transport things. Teachers can identify patterns in infants' and toddlers' play and discover ways to extend learning by observing how children manipulate materials, combine and separate materials, fit things inside containers or together, and measure materials within a space.

Chapter 5 centers on another prominent aspect of the life of infants and toddlers: movement and music. Through basic movements such as rolling, crawling, standing, climbing, or jumping, children experience different perspectives and learn about STEAM concepts related to speed, directionality, measurability, and geometry. In one example, Baumgart and Kroll describe how a child's experimentation with a wheel involves learning about force, wheels as a tool, and distance traveled. In addition, photos show an adult responsively assisting a child with her discovery. Another child is pictured exploring mathematical concepts of volume, speed, and patterns through manipulating sound. The narrative and photos work together to reveal children's self-directed STEAM learning.

An important area of STEAM learning, light, is the subject of chapter 6. We see how a teacher can encourage a child to manipulate light and use basic causal relationships to design new learning experiences. Baumgart and Kroll discuss children's construction of foundational knowledge about circuits through exploring things such as light switches. The ways children use technology, textiles, and light devices to investigate the properties of light is also examined.

In chapter 7, Baumgart and Kroll consider four aspects of the environment: *teachers' interests, children's interests, physical space,* and *culture and family contexts.* They begin by emphasizing the importance of reflection in shaping an environment that facilitates STEAM learning. A list of questions helps teachers consider their comfort level with different materials. Baumgart and Kroll suggest that a teacher's tinkering can inform how to introduce materials to infants and toddlers and connect with the children's questions about a material. The authors discuss different barriers: teachers' own attitudes, differences of opinions within teaching teams, or set routines of practice. Baumgart and Kroll then describe bridges that connect to children's learning. This chapter also honors the contributions of family and community and provides suggestions on how to make STEAM learning visible to them. Finally, both the text and photos illuminate the relationship between space and materials and the type of materials—particularly open-ended and hands on—that engage children in exploration and making discoveries.

Rich with practical concepts and suggestions, chapter 8 addresses tools, media, and materials. The authors elaborate on the meaning of *learning scripts, tinkering opportunities,* and *developing a craft.* They also discuss the teacher's role as a facilitator and extender of children's learning. A highly useful table offers questions for teachers to ask themselves about presenting media. Another table lists media that have transformative, multipurpose, and natural processes connected to them. For teachers seeking to enhance the STEAM learning in their infant and toddler settings, this chapter is invaluable.

Chapter 9 draws our attention to the dynamic nature of STEAM learning. Baumgart and Kroll explain how reflection and design work hand in hand in an infant and toddler setting. Reflection informs what kinds of designs are likely to work best in a specific learning context. The purpose of design is to address issues in the environment. The discussion ranges from cost to aesthetic considerations. One example shows a design that creatively meets the needs of children at different developmental levels. As children interact with the organized or designed space in increasingly complex ways, teachers can observe, document, and reflect on the children's learning. In addition, the authors describe and illustrate through photos children's exploration of a tool and a material separately before experiencing them together.

Chapter 10 looks toward preschool. Baumgart and Kroll underscore how a teacher's role changes. A teacher of infants and toddlers makes suggestions, wonders with the children, asks questions, introduces ideas and materials, and designs the environment based on observation, documentation, and reflection. A teacher of preschoolers supports and guides the children as they make and realize elaborate plans. As with infants and toddlers, a teacher also needs to observe, listen to, record, and represent the ideas and discoveries preschoolers wonder about and the questions they ask.

My comments hardly scratch the surface of Baumgart and Kroll's wonderful book. Studying the sequences of aesthetically pleasing photos alone would provide valuable insights to anyone interested in supporting STEAM learning of infants and toddlers. The text offers a compelling perspective on both the role of infants and toddlers in STEAM learning and the role of the teacher in facilitating their learning. It honors the active role of infants and toddlers and makes visible their natural engagement in STEAM learning. Moreover, it offers practical guidance on how teachers can organize and present learning experiences and environments that connect with infants' and toddlers' developing interests, questions, and ideas and lead to exciting possibilities to extend their learning.

—Peter Mangione, codirector for the Center
for Child and Family Studies at WestEd

Acknowledgments

I am grateful to Charlotte and Miles, Condy, and Dana, who taught me about the inventiveness and insight of young children, and Nikki Baumgart, who taught me so much about looking closely at the brilliance of babies and toddlers. I will never look at what young children are doing in the same way as I did before. I understand how everything children do is to find out how things work! I also want to thank Nikki for inviting me to participate in this exciting work.

—Linda R. Kroll

I wish to express my gratitude to Morgan, Nathaneal, and Betsy, who inspired me to share these experiences with the greater world and have guided me along this path to make this book a reality for others. This project could not have succeeded without the help of Linda R. Kroll, whose curiosity to understand children's learning is evident in everything she does. Her insightful questions and reflective stance have inspired me to notice the social and cognitive aspects of learning. I am very grateful to have Linda as a partner with me in writing this book, and I am honored that she wanted to pursue this experience with me. I also want to dedicate this book to Sergei, who has been a steady supporter, partner, and believer in me while I wrote this book.

—Nichole A. Baumgart

These acknowledgments would not be complete without the authors thanking the teachers, children, and families who have contributed to this book through their engagement with STEAM curricula and activities. Without the openness of the teachers to trying out these materials and activities, and their willingness to have observers participate in the curriculum, this book would never have been written. We also want to thank the families who engaged with us in thinking about the potential of STEAM reasoning with very young children.

Finally, we would like to acknowledge the editors and staff at Redleaf Press who saw us through this complex process. Kara Lomen was incredibly helpful as we moved through the writing process, and Rebecca Kittelson gave us wonderful editorial advice and guidance as we edited the work we had done.

Introduction

The authors of this book are two educators who have worked for a long time with both young children and teachers. Nichole Baumgart has taught children from birth to transitional kindergarten in a variety of contexts across the country. She sees herself as a learner alongside the children in the classroom and values the human development perspective that is connected to children's learning experiences. She continues to support current and prospective teachers in the early childhood and psychology fields in developing a praxis for working with young children and their families. Nichole's teaching experiences at Google's Children's Center, Mills College Children's Center, and Stanford's Bing Nursery School have shaped her thinking around the value of play, uses of technology, and the role of culture in children's learning experiences. Linda R. Kroll is a former preschool and elementary school teacher who now teaches prospective early childhood and elementary-level teachers. Her current passion is documentation as a research process and an aid to reflection and inquiry, particularly for teachers and children together. This passion allows her to observe closely many examples of the brilliance of our youngest students, and to observe how everything they do is directed at figuring out how the world works.

This book is about using Science, Technology, Engineering, the Arts, and Mathematics with very young children. STEAM is an extension of the original STEM efforts to develop scientific and mathematical thinking for use in technology and engineering with the addition of the arts and the goal to support the native creativity and innovation that all children possess. Art allows for engineers and scientists to see information differently in the ways that they perceive, understand, and deal with a given problem (Daugherty 2013). The use of STEAM (or even STEM) has not yet made much of an impact in early childhood curriculum, particularly not for the youngest children, infants and toddlers.

The teaching of science, technology, engineering, and mathematics is undergoing a change from a fact-based teaching model to a process and investigative approach. No longer is the challenge simply to find the right answer but to find and explore interesting and important questions. A goal of this change is to produce an internationally more competitive workforce that can participate in the creation of new and innovative industry.

Teachers who are not scientists or engineers may find STEM or STEAM concepts intimidating. These concepts appear in most infant and toddler activities, just waiting for teachers to make them explicit and apparent both to themselves and to the children. Infants and toddlers are continually trying to understand how their world works. As teachers, it is our responsibility to support this investigation.

Art media create a common language for children of all ages to investigate STEAM concepts. These media allow children to apply their learning to meaningful and creative contexts. Children are continuously learning about simple scientific concepts. The art media support children's extension and representation of these concepts and their creativity in their study of why the concepts are particularly important to their lived experiences. Children access the art of design in their playful exchanges, and they use elements of design to foster new ideas and individuality; children naturally involve their playful and imaginative expressions and connect them with their peer culture. This is evident when many children in a classroom setting construct similar design themes in their continuous day-after-day creations at school (for example, individually styled rockets that all have a button for food to come traveling in from space). The common culture's desire to have the "button" on their rocket ships can promote more engagement and understanding with STEAM concepts (in this case, such as cause and effect). Art media provide space for children to redesign their thinking and to apply commonly held STEM concepts to their own lived experiences and future ideas.

We see children actively constructing their learning spaces with an aesthetic approach to their learning. Children naturally do what feels right to them and build their learning in this way. They engage in a process of inquiry that highlights STEAM concept understandings through the art media. For example, some children line up their shoes in a row or put shapes together in a way that makes sense to them. They are trying to fulfill an aesthetic purpose in how they organize the objects, in addition to mathematically categorizing them by size and shape. How things look or are arranged is important to infants and toddlers. Arranging objects is a way that young children make sense of the relationships between and among objects. Their arrangements and explanations of why they arrange things the way they do provide their teachers with insight into the children's understanding.

Accessing art elements for STEAM concept learning distinguishes the difference between learning a specific function and developing a personal touch for how a function is administered. Children naturally create designs that are meaningful to them around their STEAM concept experiences. In time, their designs form a common language for children to further their STEAM concept explorations with each other. We see this when one child presents an idea in the classroom and the next day all the children want to design something similar. A common language for how children explore STEAM concepts becomes established, and children make many renditions around their common STEAM concept understandings. The element of design can entice children to explore a given STEAM concept with more enthusiasm or interest than if it were simply provided in scientific or mathematical terms. Design provides new opportunities for children to experiment with STEAM concepts as they try to better fit a different idea to their play.

You may remember a particular experience with circuits in your science class from childhood where you had to make the lightbulb light up. There was a limited set of materials, and there was only one answer to the problem. Now, imagine what this classroom experience would have been like if you had had an opportunity to design a circuit for a particular purpose rather than simply learning how to do a specific task. For example, maybe you tried to find a way to move objects across water using circuits, or maybe you wanted to create a switch box so that when your model railroad engine passed a certain point, the light went on and then at another point the light went off. These different contexts elicit varied designs leading to a similar learning experience with circuits. The experience associated with STEAM concept learning challenges children to be flexible, to take greater risks in their learning, and to make more connections related to science, mathematics, technology, engineering, and art concepts. Through time, children begin to develop a common language with one another that extends from their learning experiences into new STEAM concept discoveries. They might develop laser shooters and create different laser renditions in their future experiences with circuits. The common language, to design a medium with lasers involved, is pursued, and the classroom then engages in finding all the possible solutions to create laser circuits. Notice how the design element of art propels future discoveries and investigations with the STEAM concepts. It eliminates the previously held notion that teaching one lesson about the concept will be sufficient to ensure children's understanding of the material.

In the educational system, STEAM concepts are often used to frame a given learning experience and to provoke a learner's thinking. STEAM is a process for understanding that goes beyond knowing a defined set of facts. It is a way of thinking in which each STEAM concept is discovered in tandem with another and not teased out separately. Children in STEAM environments frequently reference combinations of science, technology, engineering, the arts, and mathematical concepts in a given learning experience. STEAM activities challenge children to find multiple solutions to a given problem and to create and confront mistakes along their learning journeys. STEAM curricula support the development of problem-solving skills, divergent thinking, interpretation of information, and the discovery of connections between the natural world and ourselves. The conscious inclusion of STEAM concepts in curricula promotes a way of thinking where thinkers design, implement, and create ideas that further human existence on earth. In this fashion, STEAM can be a way to discover, collaborate, and investigate.

Curricula based on STEAM concepts provide an integrated approach to teaching that focuses on children's processes of understanding and learning. In the early childhood field, educators can be intentional in their interactions with very young children's STEAM experiences and simultaneously support their own creative STEAM learning.

STEAM's Connection to Infants and Toddlers

Starting at birth, children have the ability to engage in STEAM concepts that will serve them throughout their lives. For example, infants and toddlers are naturally curious about how objects relate to space. They discover an object's geometric shape and properties by watching, touching, mouthing, throwing, and kicking the object. They begin to notice how one object may interact differently than another object in space, and they try to figure out under what circumstances objects behave in different ways and in interaction with each other. With time, infants and toddlers begin to construct experiences next to their peers, watching how others may be using an object to re-create their peers' experiences as their own. They may use technology to move an object by constructing a simple ramp, utilizing wheel structures, or re-adjusting a light source that projects objects onto a screen. These tangible memories are later retrieved when older children and adults abstractly visualize how an object behaves under different circumstances in a given space (Notari-Syverson and Sadler 2008), whether it is graphic arts designers creating a visual concept or architects optimizing buildings' functions and spaces.

What do the different aspects of STEAM look like in young children's thinking, problem setting, and problem solving? While we have noted that these concepts are not separately addressed by the *children*, for our own understanding and teaching, it is important to recognize and name the different concepts we observe infants and toddlers engaging with.

Science: Infants and toddlers engage in scientific concepts and investigations every day in many different contexts. When they observe or participate in preparing meals or a snack, they may notice that butter melts or that combining oatmeal and water (one wet and runny, and the other dry particles) creates a gooey, wet substance. When they go out for a walk, they gather natural materials like rocks, leaves, sticks, and seedpods. Even nonmobile babies love to hold rocks, throw rocks, and roll rocks. When they take a bath, they notice that the rocks they threw into the bathtub sank but that their bath toys float. These are all scientific observations that develop scientific understandings.

Technology: Technology can be as ordinary as basic tools that have been used in different daily activities for centuries, or it can include the technological and digital tools of our more modern era. With appropriate supervision, babies and toddlers can interact with kitchen utensils, simple hammers, nails, safe scissors, cell phones and touch-screen tablets, light switches, flashlights, radios, and televisions. All of these technologies can be used to act on the environment around them, giving infants and toddlers a sense of mastery and provoking curiosity about how things work in the world. In addition, infants and toddlers learn to use different objects for different purposes, to solve problems they have set for themselves. Jean Piaget (1962) shares an example of his daughter as a baby, in a playpen, using a stick to pull an object that is beyond her reach toward her.

Engineering: Engineering concepts involve understanding how different objects and technologies relate to one another and how those relationships can contribute to making something new out of different pieces. Toddlers build with blocks, construct weapons out of sticks, use one object to support another, and build structures that then are used to represent other things. They also use objects to solve problems they have set for themselves.

The Arts and Design: Experimenting with natural materials and qualities, such as texture, color, shape, smell, taste, sound, and movement, are all aspects of art and design concepts. Babies enjoy experimenting with materials and tools, which they will later use to represent their ideas and rerepresent their understandings and thinking (when they are older). But early experiences with artistic media and creating something new out of disparate parts contribute to the construction of art and design concepts.

Mathematics: Mathematical concepts include number, order, geometric shapes, classes of objects, and patterns. Babies and young children are aware of greater and lesser amounts, enjoy lining things up to compare them, create patterns with objects, and learn to sort things by their different characteristics. Sorting by different characteristics begins from birth, as babies learn different ways to act on the world around them—what things can be sucked or not sucked, what things can be grasped or pinched, and so forth.

Infants' and toddlers' general learning stance lends itself naturally to STEAM ways of thinking in which learning is constructed through tinkering, cause and effect, observations, and experimentation, and by doing or "making." Their persistent tendency to test, retest, and re-create previous experiences with objects is comparable to how a tester might approach troubleshooting a given problem. Very young children may not be able to verbally share their thinking about STEAM concepts, but they can display these same understandings and more in the ways that they approach and interact with their worlds. Teachers can connect with these infant and toddler STEAM understandings by observing the ways that infants and toddlers interact with objects in their environments and by modifying the children's environments to expand on their natural learning moments.

Throughout the past decade, there have been many resources, trainings, and shifts in educational philosophies to include STEM (not STEAM) experiences within the K–12 education system, but little attention has been given to either set of concepts in early childhood education. Intentional, simple technology experiences serving as active tools for children to participate and learn about STEAM concepts are just emerging in the early childhood field. These recent technology advancements have not achieved their potential in the very early childhood setting, partly because the STEAM knowledge of early childhood educators is not recognized by either their directors or themselves. Early childhood educators may have more limited experiences in designing specific STEAM activities for their students and may not recognize their own STEAM knowledge. We will discuss ways to meet this challenge and overcome these hesitancies throughout the book.

In this book, we discuss how STEAM concepts support young children's cognitive and social development, and how these concepts appear in everything they do to learn about their world. We share a pedagogical framework that draws on this perspective to show how curriculum and environment can be organized to support this development. In addition, we explore the following questions:

- How do we make visible children's STEAM learning and concept development?

- How do educators facilitate, reflect, and respond to children's work in STEAM concepts?

- What environments further support infants' and toddlers' explorations of STEAM concepts?

How to Use This Book

This book is organized into three sections. The first section (this introduction and chapter 1) introduces the book and discusses infant and toddler learning and development in relationship to STEAM concepts. The second section (chapters 2–6) is a series of examples of STEAM curricula in infant and toddler classrooms. These vignettes encompass different learning environments and materials, all of which contribute to STEAM concept development. Each vignette presents a scenario of infant and toddler learning and engagement with STEAM concepts and activities. These vignettes help the reader think about a particular aspect of STEAM curriculum and how a teacher might build a larger curricular unit using these concepts and materials. Each vignette is an example of a learning story and demonstrates how these instances provide a spark for the teacher and the child to continue and deepen the exploration of the particular materials and concepts. These chapters end with questions to consider in extending and reflecting on the events described. The final section (chapters 7–9) focuses on classroom environments and setting up a context for effective development of STEAM curricula for teachers and effective STEAM concept learning for infants and toddlers. This section concludes with a peek at what will follow in preschool classrooms, building on what has been developed through the curricula and learning stances described here for babies and toddlers (chapter 10).

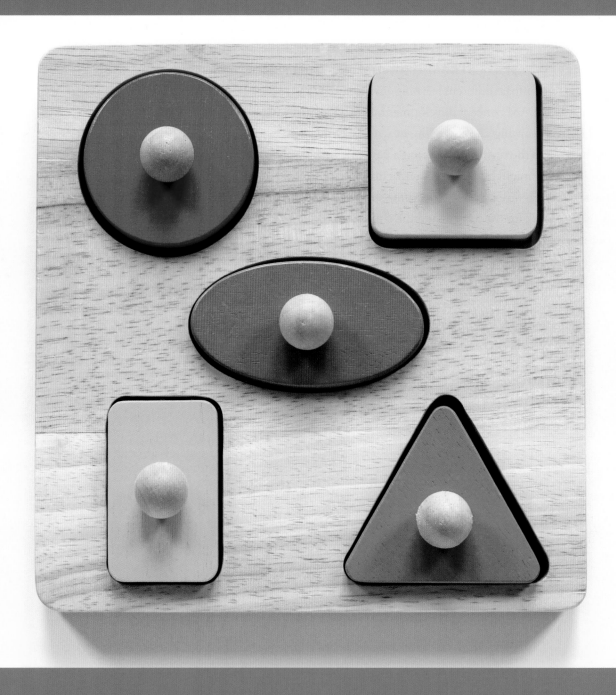

Chapter 1

Infants and Toddlers
STEAM Learning from the Beginning of Life

NEW ACADEMIC PRESSURES to educate children to be more creative and innovative emphasize the improvement of instruction in science and mathematics. The pressure to increase the number of students entering the fields of science, technology, engineering, and mathematics has resulted in a rash of curricula focused on STEM subject matter. More recently, the insertion of the arts into these curricula has been suggested as a way to be more inclusive of the variety of talents and interests that students have, as well as to provide more possible perspectives in thinking creatively about our world. Noticeably absent is any reference to the education of infants and toddlers in thinking about these content areas.

There are some examples of STEAM curricula in early childhood education. Developmental psychologist Rheta DeVries and her colleagues' (2002) work in constructivist education emphasizes the introduction of scientific questions or wonderings into the early childhood classroom. Specifically, she looks at how children develop their understandings of physical knowledge (as defined by Jean Piaget). For example, her elaborate unit on the use of ramps for children to explore concepts of engineering (building elaborate ramp structures), gravity (recognizing that for the cars to go, they need to roll down the ramp), scientific prediction (where I place the car determines where it will end up on a ramp), and so forth gives young children vast opportunities for systematically discovering how the physical world works in different circumstances (DeVries and Sales 2011). Earlier work by Constance Kamii and DeVries (1993) examines the value of incorporating physical knowledge activities into preschool curriculum, where these activities provide children the opportunity to observe, interact with, and cause changes in objects through building, actions, and representation. Incorporating the arts into scientific investigation, developmental psychologists Carolyn Hildebrandt and Betty Zan (DeVries, Zan, et al. 2002) provided children with the opportunity to explore the physics of sound while creating musical instruments for composing music. In Reggio Emilia programs, children create different representations of their ideas as they deepen and broaden their understanding of these ideas. The systematic and repeated use of representation in multiple media incorporates design and artistic representation into exploration of physical phenomena. For example, in the creation of an amusement park for birds, children represented a city fountain and its inner workings through drawing and clay and in multiple layers on Lucite and visual projection (Gandini 2012).

How such explorations might manifest themselves in the infant and toddler classroom is an important question. Again, in Reggio Emilia programs, eighteen-month-old children explore the nature of time, using an hourglass and a camera, thus drawing on both scientific and artistic reasoning and understanding (Reggio Children 2011). Swedish researcher Hillevi Lenz-Taguchi (2010) describes infants' systematic and carefully orchestrated experiences with floating and sinking, leading to a far more advanced understanding of the phenomenon than is typically observed.

Infant and Toddler Learning

We begin with what we know about how babies and toddlers learn and what environments and experiences contribute to that learning. Research shows that infants are actively investigating their world from the moment they are born (Maguire-Fong 2015). How developmental psychologists have researched these investigations and then reported them has changed over the years, but there is no question that babies are putting together information about the world around them, in systematic ways, from the moment of birth.

Developmental psychologist Alison Gopnik (2009, 2012) describes current research that shows that the process used by young children to test and form hypotheses is similar to the process used by adult scientists. Swiss psychologists Jean Piaget and Bärbel Inhelder (Piaget and Inhelder 1974) describe infants and toddlers' learning as sensorimotor, in that all of the thinking that is going on is observable in the children's actions. They describe systematic experimentation and repeated attempts that they interpret as infants constructing an understanding of how the world around them works, particularly with regard to objects and object relations, space, time, and causality, all "scientific" and "mathematical" concepts. While many have used Piaget's work to show what infants *cannot* do, it is useful to use his work to show what infants *can* do, and to demonstrate that toddlers make amazing advances in their thinking when they are given a variety of opportunities to interact with materials and activities repeatedly. Building on Inhelder and Piaget's work, theorists have demonstrated that infants make sense of the world differently than Piaget concluded. For example, child psychologist Renée Baillargeon (1994) examines what infants know about hidden objects and the expectations that they have about objects based on what they know about them. She contends that Piaget's ideas underestimate or misinterpret what babies know or are able to figure out. While it is not our purpose here to dispute the work of either researcher, their work supports our ideas about what is possible and therefore reasonable to think about in teaching infants and toddlers with STEAM curricula and activities.

Areas of Development

Researchers tend to focus on different aspects of development depending on their particular interests or research questions. However, all developmental researchers understand that each area of development is closely related to the other areas, and that while we may talk about these areas individually, we understand that they affect one another. Piaget and Inhelder (1974) wrote about the relationship between affective, cognitive, and social development, concluding that emotional development and motivation are the engine that drives the rest of development. More recent research is not as specific in relating one aspect of development to another. How development is divided is also not universally agreed upon; nevertheless, for our purposes it is useful to consider each area briefly in relation to how babies and toddlers learn. The different areas include emotional, physical, social, language, and cognitive development; however, *all* aspects of development are influenced by the culture in which the child is born and cared for. Thus, in discussing the different aspects of development, keeping in mind the cultural nature of human development is paramount (Rogoff 2003).

Emotional

Emotional development begins before birth. In the best of circumstances, babies are cared for from their conception. When they are born, their behaviors endear them to their caretakers, creating a bond that attaches the child to their caretakers. While most research in the field of *attachment* looks at relationships between the mother and child, children can attach to multiple adults early on (Ainsworth 1982; Bowlby 1969). From the beginning, emotional development is tied to mutually constructed social relationships. When these relationships are stable and responsive, the baby feels secure and cared for. She can then go out from this secure base to explore the rest of the world.

Routines and rituals can contribute to STEAM understanding as well. For example, when a baby's diaper is changed or she is settled for nursing (two very early routines), the baby comes to recognize where these activities take place, making sense of her spatial surroundings. The construction of the space associated with different activities is related to developing a recognitory scheme for one's surroundings. ("I'm in this place, so this familiar ritual of diaper changing is going to take place—thank goodness since I'm so *wet!*"). In this space, you can have intimate social interaction with the baby—looking directly into her face and responding to her cues. Making sense of the space in which she finds herself, the baby constructs a scheme about her surroundings. When new things are placed in the environment, or when typical activities are carried out in strange surroundings, the baby recognizes the difference.

Other routines can involve leaving and returning, encouraging the development of the notion of object permanence—that when someone is no longer visible, that does not mean she is no longer there. Babies respond with delight to games of peekaboo, indicating that they recognize both the disappearance of the adult player and the certainty of their reappearance. Research conducted by Baillargeon (1994) demonstrates that young babies from early on recognize that if things are not seen, it does not mean they no longer exist. Making sense of the geography of their surroundings is an essential scientific and mathematical understanding that is developed early by infants. Rituals and routines contribute to this understanding.

Physical

When we think about physical development in relation to STEAM learning, what is perhaps most salient is babies' developing abilities to interact independently with the environment. At first, babies can only handle and interact with objects that you give them or show them. As they develop greater strength and coordination, they become more able to handle objects and use different grips to interact with objects. They can move from lying down to sitting up, to standing up; each of these different positions provides a different perspective on the world and a new opportunity to interact with their surroundings.

Social

Social development is closely entwined with emotional development. Human beings have evolved to be social beings. The social nature of people is part of survival and part of the biological and cultural heritage of humans. Babies expect to be cared for and are programmed from the beginning to respond to other people. They are attracted to faces and know from the beginning how to scan a face and how to connect with one. They respond to familiar smells (their mother or other caregiver), sounds (the sound of familiar voices), and likenesses (people they "know") by settling down or responding with the intent gaze of interest.

Interaction with other people occurs from the moment of birth. Babies are interested in people early on, and adults and other children are equally interesting. In one example, a two-month-old baby and a fifteen-month-old toddler were facing each other at a dinner party (both held by their grandmothers). The two-month-old had been fussing and generally not happy in his situation; the fifteen-month-old had been trying to get down on the floor. When he saw the younger baby, he stopped struggling, and his face lit up in a smile; simultaneously, the younger baby settled down and looked intently at the older baby. They both found each other interesting and recognized each other in some fundamental way.

Infant and toddler learning is rooted in social interactions. The child and the caregiver exchange cues that encourage behavior on the part of both participants. Caregivers react to positive responses from babies, and babies respond to loving and caring behavior from their grown-ups. As children get older and more independent physically from their surroundings—they learn to sit up, crawl, reach for things, pull up, scoot after things they want, and walk—they interact with their environment in a number of ways. The environment is provided by the caregivers and is culturally and socially constructed. Within the environment there are multiple opportunities for consciously including STEAM activities. But many of them already exist and, once recognized, can be extended. For example, seating a baby on a large piece of paper with a marker allows the baby multiple opportunities for exploring technology (the marker as tool) or for seeing color and making colorful marks connected to her movements (art and design). Doing this activity together shows the baby other possibilities for using the marker and other possible results. This is not direction but rather opportunity for observation and experimentation in a socially supportive situation.

In addition, babies often create these opportunities for themselves. A sixteen-month-old toddler shows his two train cars that connect via magnets to a new adult. The adult responds by demonstrating the attraction and repulsion of the train cars (depending on their orientation to one another). The toddler watches and then takes the two cars to show them to another new adult. Both adults respond with language and demonstration, and the toddler is clearly interested in both making social contact with these new people and demonstrating something of interest. Magnetic attraction and repulsion is an interesting scientific phenomenon that violates our expectations about what is commonly observed as relations between objects.

Language

The period of infancy and toddlerhood is crucial for language development. Infants begin to comprehend language first in a global sense and later in a particular sense as they recognize the people who speak to them and learn to attend to their speech. Within the first year of life, babies learn to communicate with their caregivers through gesture and vocalization. By the end of the first year, babies wave bye-bye, point to specific things, and understand several phrases (such as "Give Mama a hug," "Let's go bye-bye," and "Do you want a bottle?"), all signs of language comprehension. Miles, at eleven months, understood when his grandmother said to him, "Let's take a bath." He would head for the bathroom and pull himself up on the bathtub, trying to dive in, clothes and all.

During the second year, children learn many words and phrases and gradually develop the ability to articulate these words and phrases. When adults name and label things and actions, they are supporting children's understanding of how the world is organized and, simultaneously, providing them with a system of naming what they have already understood. STEAM concepts are represented in children's beginning language by identifying objects and actions and providing children with the sign or symbol for a particular object or action. By the end of the second year, many children use complex sentences to express ideas and to talk about things that are not in front of them or immediately evident. Thus, language supports the child's ability to talk about and represent the world even when items or actions are not immediately present. You tell the toddler, "We are going to school now," and he runs to the door and says, "car," indicating not only that he knows what is about to happen, but also that he has a complex scheme for what "going to school" entails. Toddlers learn words for amount, like "more" or "two," and demonstrate their understanding of these mathematical terms when they ask for "more" or note that they have "two" of something. Language development is an important aspect of all other strands of development as it supports social, emotional, and cognitive learning and is in turn supported by these strands.

Many children are learning more than one language at once. For these children, developing productive language may seem to take a bit longer. However, they understand both languages they are hearing from just as early an age as children who are learning only one language. The more they are exposed to both languages, the more they learn both to understand and, ultimately, speak them. In this dual-language learning process, they have one advantage over monolingual children: they are learning that one concept or object may be represented by more than one word or phrase. This diversity of labels gives them an advantage in problem solving, since there can be more than one answer to a problem.

Cognitive

What does cognitive development look like early on, and what are babies born with? There is an ongoing debate regarding this question. Nevertheless, from birth, babies are figuring out their surroundings and their world. Piaget described this period of cognitive development as the sensorimotor period, implying that babies do not yet have mental representation available to them, and thus all their thinking is done through action, building on the reflexes with which they are born. Since Piaget's groundbreaking work almost a century ago, researchers, using a variety of technological tools and the violation-of-expectations method, have conducted studies that show infants may have representational competence, along with basic conceptual reasoning, earlier on than previously thought (Lightfoot, Cole, and Cole 2013). No matter how early, it is clear that infancy and toddlerhood is a period of great cognitive growth, as babies become problem-posing, problem-solving individuals, learning from their cultural environments to use tools, to explore their surroundings, and to make connections in the cognitive areas of space, time, causality, object permanence, characteristics, and relationships. Piaget characterizes the way infants (and all people for that matter) construct knowledge as the development of schemes of action, whether they be motor or mental schemes. Schemes begin as an adaptation and refinement of the basic reflexes, but babies quickly adapt these schemes. Piaget (1969) describes this adaptation as an interaction of assimilation and accommodation. As babies have the opportunity to act on their environment, they develop more complex schemes.

> Thirteen-month-old Miles slips his small toy tiger between the slats of a coffee table. He crawls around the corner of the table to retrieve the tiger, but he can't reach it. He returns to the slatted side and reaches in and grabs it. Then, he repeats the action, putting the tiger through the slats. This time, when he crawls around to the open side, he reaches in farther, but he still can't reach it because he cannot get his head under the table at all (he is on his knees rather than his belly). His grandfather watches him, then gets down next to him, stretches out on his belly, and reaches in, saying, "See, just reach in." Miles watches him attentively, then goes down on *his* belly, reaches in just a little bit farther, and retrieves the tiger. He goes around the table and repeats his action, putting the tiger through the slats and then retrieving it on the open side.

Miles has created a problem to solve for himself, figuring out the spatial relationships between himself, the structure of the table, and the position of the toy. He repeats the action, varying where he places the toy under the table and retrieving it from both sides of the table. He has created a complex scheme for where he, the table, and the toy are in space in relationship to one another. He is also able to learn from watching a model perform the action he wants to complete, indicating some variety of mental representation no matter how fleeting that representation may be. How we position ourselves in space and how we interact with the objects in that space are basic to understanding scientific and engineering concepts.

Another way to interpret this example is through a more Vygotskian lens. Lev Vygotsky (and other social constructivists) point out that all knowledge is constructed in collaboration with others. In this instance, Miles's grandfather sees the problem the baby is having (not realizing that his head and back are blocking his ability to reach in far enough to get the toy) and demonstrates a solution to the problem. Clearly this demonstration is right in Miles's zone of proximal development (ZPD; Vygotsky 1978) since as soon as he sees his grandfather go down on his belly, he imitates him and is able to reach in farther under the table. This is a lovely example of the interaction between the adult and baby supporting the baby's independence and development. Again, they are interacting around a scientific and engineering concept of space and relations within space.

Types of Knowledge

Piaget described three types of knowledge: physical knowledge, logico-mathematical knowledge, and social knowledge (Kamii and DeVries 1993). Infants and toddlers construct all of these forms of knowledge, but the mode of construction is different for each one. In physical knowledge, the individual builds schemes of understanding through acting directly on the objects and experiencing their physical properties. In logico-mathematical knowledge, we construct understandings by putting what we have learned (either through physical knowledge construction or social construction or a combination of both) into relationships with one another. Thus, aspects of an object, such as its shape, color, taste, and so forth, are formed as physical knowledge, but aspects such as number, size, order, or pattern are formed through logico-mathematical knowledge. "This red ball is bigger than this yellow one." The color of the balls is physical knowledge, and the size comparison is logico-mathematical knowledge. The names or labels for physical aspects (such as shape or color) are logico-mathematical knowledge in that they are created through the interaction of physical and social knowledge. Social knowledge is constructed with other people. Babies and toddlers learn culturally specific information through social knowledge, most notably language and behavioral expectations. Developing comprehension and, later producing language enable babies to participate socially in interaction with other people and with their surroundings. As adults (and older children) speak *to* babies, the babies respond to these attempts at communication and connection, seeking to interpret what is being communicated. Specifically, what is communicated as social knowledge is the result of cultural construction of particular knowledge for different communities. Early childhood educator Mary Jane Maguire-Fong (2015, 25) notes that "patterns of eye contact between adult and child, terms and gestures of respect and deference, ways of transporting infants (e.g., in slings, in strollers, in backpacks), or the pattern of discourse—all influence how infants behave and, in turn, how infants expect others to behave."

From the beginning, babies are building all three kinds of STEAM knowledge. As babies refine their physical coordination, learning to reach for, grasp, suck, and otherwise handle objects, they are building physical knowledge of those objects. As they learn to differentiate, to adapt their physical actions toward different objects, they are also creating categories of objects—these are suckable, these are not; these can be grabbed with the whole hand, these require a pincer grip; there are two of these; they can be lined up, organized in a variety of ways. This physical differentiation also includes logico-mathematical knowledge as the babies are comparing the objects to one another. As Maguire-Fong (2015, 24) says, "In simple moments of play, infants apply their expanding repertoire of physical knowledge to build an expanding repertoire of logico-mathematical knowledge."

> Ten-month-old Charlotte loves her pacifier. She places it inside a plastic ring from her stacking rings toy. Then, she lifts up the ring, with the pacifier pointing in toward her, and puts the pacifier in her mouth. She repeats this action several times, each time being more successful and adept at the coordination of pacifier and ring.

Here Charlotte is using the ring as a tool; she is using two schemes that she practices regularly, putting one thing inside another and putting her pacifier in her mouth, in combination. The two schemes represent physical knowledge, while the connection she has made between these two schemes is logico-mathematical knowledge. The ring becomes a tool for achieving a goal that she has achieved previously but represents her use of technology in novel forms.

STEAM in the Environment

Naturally occurring opportunities for STEAM investigations are all around us; babies seek them out as they figure out their world. They experiment with gravity as they knock down a tower of blocks. They experiment with object permanence and space as they send a toy train into a tunnel and look for it to come out, first at the end they put it in, and then, with more experience, at the other end. They experiment with electricity as they notice the light that goes on in the car when the door is open and then notice that it disappears. While they do not necessarily connect it with the open door, they look for it as they get into the car and notice when it disappears; turning lights on and off fascinates them. As they learn to feed themselves, they experiment with spoons and forks, trying different ways to use these tools successfully. In this day of cell phones and tablets, they learn early on to swipe and touch the screen, getting it to change, a very technological example. Paying attention to these examples and others of infants' and toddlers' naturally occurring interest in STEAM concepts and thinking about how to extend their explorations to support further development of their knowledge construction are what this book is about.

Some of the most productive opportunities for learning occur when we make mistakes or fail to achieve a goal we have set for ourselves. When a baby is learning to feed himself, he first uses his hands. But soon he is eager to try to use the utensils by himself. When he first tries to use the spoon, he will grasp the spoon in many different ways. Sometimes he will grab the handle; sometimes he will grab the bowl of the spoon. Sometimes the spoon will be right side up and the food will stay on the spoon long enough for him to get it to his mouth. Sometimes he will invert the spoon, so the food falls out. When it is upside down and the food falls out, the baby fails to feed himself. (Frequently, he will revert to using his hands when this happens.) However, through repeated attempts, he learns the most effective position for the spoon and the food to be successful. The mistakes he experiences teach him about the relationship between the orientation of the spoon, the spoon acting as a container for the food and the most effective way to get the food to his mouth. "Failure" is not discouraging; it is an opportunity to learn more complex aspects of a situation.

A notable example of exploring the ideas of floating and sinking is described by Hillevi Lenz-Taguchi (2010, 78–81). Most children have experiences with floating objects (in the bathtub with bath toys). In this case, one-year-olds were given the opportunity to experiment with floating and sinking, in pairs, in a specifically constructed environment, using clear bowls of water and a wide variety of objects. According to Lenz-Taguchi, the children were interested both in what they were doing and what their partner was doing. They closely observed their own and one another's results. They noticed and commented through gestures when something floated (sticks, leaves, small toys) and when something sank (rocks, metal objects, small tools), expressing surprise and delight. Teachers reported that the understanding of what would sink and what would float was exhibited by these toddlers when later on they encountered puddles outside. While they did not verbalize "wood things float and stones sink," the children who had had the floating and sinking experiences clearly had classified things as "sinkers" and "floaters." A typical Piagetian task is to give children the opportunity to classify objects as floaters and sinkers and then to try them out. Piaget's data do not include children as young as those children in Lenz-Taguchi's study (Inhelder and Piaget 1958). However, given this extended and purposeful experience, the babies had created these categories and were able to apply them in different contexts. Such experiences with STEAM concepts build on children's naturally occurring curiosity and investigation. The challenge for you is to create contexts that allow for their further exploration. It is not about correct answers or specific knowledge but rather about content exploration in safe and supervised contexts. It is also about close and informed observation on your part to determine *what* babies and toddlers might be wondering about, and providing opportunities for further exploration.

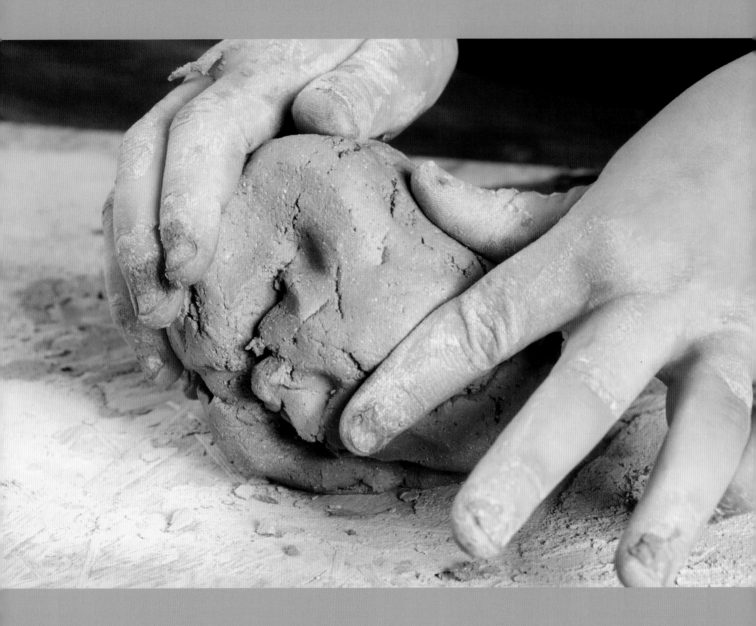

Chapter 2

Engaging in
STEAM Concepts
Working with Clay

CLAY IS A NATURAL earth medium that humans have used for centuries for multiple purposes, and it continues to be used in our modern world. Technologies that have arisen from clay have been integrated into people's daily living experiences and cultural identity formations. Art museums often picture many different clay pieces that people used in the past to collect water, to serve and cook food, and to create beads for jewelry making. Exposing children to clay at an early age allows them to gain a practical relationship with this commonly used material; in addition, it can serve as a platform for adults to learn more about children's scientific learning. Experiences with clay can further very young children's innate desire for discovery, inquiry, and curiosity.

Serving as a strong platform for very young children's explorations of STEAM concepts, clay is a transformative, open-ended material that can be used for multiple purposes. Careful attention and planning to how clay is introduced to infants and toddlers can result in activities that engage infants and toddlers in a meaning-making journey. This journey gives infants and toddlers time to grasp STEAM concepts that are connected to their own interests. The journey encompasses a series of dyadic exchanges, during which one moment experienced with clay can challenge very young children's previously held thinking about specific STEAM concepts.

Infant Clay Experience: A Social Approach

In this chapter, we highlight the adult caregiver role in facilitating infants' and toddlers' STEAM understandings and concept development. We use vignettes of interactions and play with clay to further explain how infants and toddlers access STEAM concepts through play with clay. Concluding our chapter, we discuss how these STEAM understandings are expanded on in toddlerhood.

> Amir's connections to clay's mathematical and scientific properties are embedded in a social approach. An eight-month-old infant, Amir is experiencing clay with his family in their child care setting for the first time. While sitting in his father's lap, Amir first observes his teachers and peers interact with the clay. During this time, Amir sees Danika leave her parent's arms and quickly crawl straight over to the cube of clay; she begins to slap the clay very loudly as if it were a drum. The clay responds with a solid sound as Danika props herself up on the clay block and pats the top of it. Amir's eyes gaze intently at the gray clay cube and Danika's hands. Soon more infants approach the block, and Amir starts to lean forward toward the clay while still remaining in his father's lap. Some of the other infants begin to poke the clay with their fingers and stare at the newly formed marks on the clay.
>
> After watching for a bit more time, Amir's father places Amir onto his stomach near the clay cube and sits down next to him. Amir's body is relaxed, but he does not touch the clay. Instead, Amir looks intently at the marks created by the other infants. He notices new marks being

Danika pinches the clay and creates ridged marks on the clay.

formed as he witnesses his peers pass their fingers along the clay. Amir follows these lines along the clay block and looks up at his father. His father gestures to Amir that it is okay for him to touch the clay. Amir smiles and remains still, all the while staring at his father. His father gently touches the clay near Amir's space, and Amir reaches out to the block of clay at that very moment. Their hands touch each other as the clay rests beneath them.

Amir references his father while touching the clay block.

Amir manipulates the clay block with his fingers.

Amir shares his new discovery with his peers around him after looking at the broken piece of clay.

Amir holds his hand on the block and begins to curl his fingers. He looks back to reference his father. When he completely curls up his fingers, a small piece of clay becomes stuck on his fingertips. Amir does not seem bothered by this and spreads out his hands again. After Amir curls his fingers once more, the piece of clay falls down to the canvas near his face. He stares at the fallen piece and scoots his body forward to get a better look. He lifts up the clay piece and holds it in front of him as pulls himself up to a kneeling position. Pieces of the clay break and fall onto the ground. He continues staring intently at his clenched hands holding the initial piece of scraped-off clay.

In this vignette, Amir notices the effect that he has on a solid block of clay after he has had time to adjust and feel comfortable in approaching the clay. Strong attachment bonds with family and caregivers can further support children's STEAM concept explorations because they give infants and toddlers a secure place from which to explore their environment independently. When children feel safe, they are more willing to take risks in their thinking, exploring, and manipulating of raw materials.

Amir actively participates in his experiences with clay by observation. He notices the cause-and-effect relationships happening when his peers manipulate the clay. With each observation, Amir gains a stronger sense of the clay's properties and the ways that clay can be manipulated. His peers and father modeled strategies to touch the clay, and he uses these observations to formulate his own approach to touching the clay.

In these simple observations, Amir is connecting his scientific understandings as he imitates an artist's technique for sculpting the clay while considering the clay's physical properties. He experiments and makes predictions as to how he can alter the clay's solid form by repeatedly curling his fingers. Notice that Amir does not expect the clay to spread out like a liquid or to move quickly like a light medium. Instead, he intentionally touches the sturdy block of clay with his fingers and stares at the already formed marks. He has understood that something happened to create these marks on the cube, and he is interested in investigating how to do that himself. These are the early moments where infants begin to express themselves in an artifact form.

When Amir investigates, he is using his STEAM concept thinking because he is designing an approach to find a simple answer. He is strategizing a way to use the available medium (clay) to learn more about mark making and transformation. He experiments with the ways he can touch the clay and repeatedly tries actions that fit his thinking. He is also referencing past experiences with other media to inform how he can manipulate this new experience. Amir's previous experiences with grabbing a random assortment of objects have helped him build a schema of ways to touch larger objects in comparison to small handheld ones. Sometimes unexpected events happen that create disequilibrium in an infant's understanding of a STEAM concept. Infants may expect a certain situation to occur, and then something different transpires. In Amir's clay encounter, he witnesses a piece of the clay fall away from the clay block. Although Amir was not initially trying to understand what occurred, he examines the fallen piece of clay further and shifts his attention toward it. This open approach to clay broadens Amir's mathematical understanding through his intimate explorations of "parts to whole" concepts in his play after the piece of clay has broken off the large block. In his examination, Amir notices the different shape, texture, and size of the broken piece of clay. Amir experiences for the first time what it feels like to hold a piece of clay that fits into his hands, unlike the larger clay slab nearby. He expresses his understandings about clay by moving his body so he can see the smaller piece of clay more easily and by continuing to revisit the clay's breakable and transformative properties over and over again. Amir builds an experiential relationship to size and shape by using multiple perspectives as he first notices the piece of clay below him on the ground and later holds the clay above him to get a better look.

Amir is not only building a relationship with the clay, he is also building interconnected relationships within the STEAM concepts. Initially, Amir's observations give him a lot of information but not the experience of touching the clay. What he doesn't know is what happens during the tactile experience of working with clay: What happens when the clay is touched? How much pressure does one need to apply to make a mark? How can one break off a piece of clay? Amir's simple yet significant beginning experience with clay will serve as a tool as he encounters clay in the future. The play with clay shapes how Amir will approach new experiences and may spark new interests. Maybe next time he will notice even smaller pieces of broken clay or investigate music and movements with the clay block like Danika did. As Amir experiences clay repeatedly, he can use his strong understanding of clay to create more complex investigations and experiences with this natural medium. His connection with clay may lead him to investigate concepts centered on pressure, force, temperature, density, and more.

Expanding Infants' Experiences with Clay in Toddlerhood

Toddlers' experiences can differ slightly from infant experiences because toddlers may have had more experiences manipulating and storing information. Infants are becoming familiar with the clay medium and are discovering how the clay works. In infancy and toddlerhood, children expand on their previous skills and experiences to challenge their thinking, movements, and social connections with others. Infants and toddlers are interested in what their peers are doing, and they may try to imitate their peers' thinking or doing. Toddlers begin to expand on their peers' play and to formulate parallel play with their peers. The clay becomes more a material of shared focus than it was previously when the children were infants. Toddlers are able to make different hand movements with added force as they roll, press, squeeze, and poke the clay with greater ease. Additionally, toddlers can remember more information and can perform more sequenced tasks in a given revisited experience.

As toddlers broaden their clay experiences, they may begin to show representational images with the clay. They may narrate stories associated with their clay pieces, creating symbolic marks on their clay, or they may create a three-dimensional representation of an object. They may want to pursue an idea but realize that they need help to do it, requiring them to reach out to their peers to collaborate. With each change in or expanded approach to clay, adults are able to see children's growth in learning about STEAM concepts and be with their children every step of the way along their journey of understanding of the clay medium.

Providing these clay experiences allows infants and toddlers to develop a disposition toward construction/deconstruction, acquisition of knowledge through the senses, spatial use, and other STEAM concepts; such encounters provide an integrated and built-upon experience with a common material. This opportunity allows children to transfer their previous knowledge about balance, gravity, technology, and art to approach other media because they now have an experience exploring these STEAM concepts with clay. Taking a reflective and observant role during children's clay experiences can lead to long-term project investigations with clay and other materials, and to intimate STEAM experiences with very young children.

Technology and Engineering: Solving Problems with Tools and Materials

As the infants and toddlers observe, they begin to see how adults use technology to further their clay experiences. *Technology* can be defined as a simple tool that is used to enhance people's daily living practices or play. In infants' and toddlers' first experiences with clay, they witness clay being stored inside airtight containers and the laying of canvas underneath the clay. After repeated experiences, an educator could change the clay's shape with a wire cutter or other tool in front of the children. Infants and toddlers may have noticed an educator moistening the clay by using a spray bottle to apply water to the clay. With time, infants and toddlers begin to act on their understandings of technology. They start to open containers, manipulate the clay, explore tools, and eventually use the clay to achieve purposes in their play.

Many times infants and toddlers want to touch or do what their caregivers are doing. Providing tools separately from the clay, like clean spray bottles with small amounts of water and clean clay tools for infants to manipulate or mouth, allows infants and toddlers to use technology before they can fully apply the tools to the clay. Clay tools are introduced in a simple, intentional manner and presented with a strong purpose. How an adult first models using the tools in front of the children can provide mental images of how the tools can be used in connection with future materials. Giving infants and toddlers time to explore clay and tools separately provides them opportunities to utilize their tools and clay in tandem with specific media or directed purposes.

Infants and toddlers naturally hold an engineer's perspective as they investigate their worlds and solve problems in their play. Engineers solve everyday problems by developing and designing materials or tools for use in many situations. The establishment of strong relationships to tools and clay allows very young children to begin engineering which tools work best for a given purpose. Often infants and toddlers

Dylan is putting clay in and out of the container, a practice he sees each time an adult introduces and cleans up the clay.

Toddlers can use pins, tools, or wooden sticks to create deeper holes in their clay slabs.

will integrate their previous scientific understandings of clay to better support their future uses of clay. For example, toddlers may discover how to create a clay ball by rolling the clay around on a tabletop and then later make representational clay eggs for a nearby bird's nest they are studying. In this way, infants and toddlers are engineering possible outcomes and visual designs for their future learning experiences about a given topic.

Toddler Clay Experiences: Engineering and Collaboration

Toddlers like to move and transport objects as they investigate the different ways they can use the materials. They have established some sort of understanding of familiar materials, and they can use this knowledge to think more about how materials collide, connect, complement, or are distinguished from each other. In the vignette below, two toddlers are learning how to problem solve together to create a tall cubed tower with their available resources in their play.

Dylan begins stacking the clay cubes on top of each other while sitting on his teacher's lap.

Dylan sits next to his teacher as he stacks clay cubes on top of each other. His classmate Kieran is nearby, at the other end of the canvas, manipulating the clay cubes presented in front of him. Kieran tries to place his third clay cube on top of his tower. He carefully attempts to center the piece before releasing his grip from the cube. Dylan notices Kieran's high tower. He observes Kieran's approach and imitates what Kieran is doing. Just as Dylan tries to put on his third cube, his stacked cubes of clay fall down. Kieran observes Dylan's cubed tower fall, and he starts to move closer to Dylan. Dylan, who sometimes likes to work independently from his peers, allows Kieran to come near him, and Kieran picks up the fallen pieces of clay with his hands. Kieran begins stacking the clay cubes in front of Dylan to rebuild Dylan's fallen tower. Kieran is careful to use a similar slow motion while stacking, like he did before with his original tower. However, the tower is not sturdy, and the clay pieces fall down again. The two toddlers look at each other and burst into laughter, before swiping their arms across in front of them to knock over any remaining stacked cubes from the broken tower.

A nearby teacher notices that Kieran and Dylan might need some encouragement. She asks the two toddlers if they want to try it again. The children respond positively, and they seem engaged with the stacking activity when the teacher places two more cubes on top of each other in Kieran and Dylan's shared workspace. Kieran leans in to grab a nearby cube while Dylan quickly moves away from the space; he ventures into a different classroom space. It seems that Dylan has changed his mind about participating in this activity, but the teacher remains supportive of Kieran's stacking.

After a few minutes, Dylan returns with a new object in his hand. He has found a small wooden cube in the classroom's construction area, and he places this cube on top of the clay tower. Dylan's eyes widen. The teacher reflects and notes that they do not usually encourage mixing other classroom materials in with the clay because these materials might become damaged. Yet Dylan has solved the problem of the falling clay towers by finding a different kind of cube to use. Recognizing Dylan's big idea, the teacher narrates to Kieran that Dylan thought this wooden cube would work well for stacking.

A series of back-and-forth exchanges occurs in which one toddler puts a clay cube on the stack while the other puts a wooden cube on top of the stacked tower. The clay sticks to the wood, especially when it is pressed hard on the wood surface. Pieces of clay remain on the wooden cubes when the clay cubes are pulled off the wooden blocks. The children are attentive to these situations and continue their building together.

Dylan constructs a tall tower.

Dylan and Kieran's fallen tower.

In this vignette, the toddlers display how learning about STEAM concepts happens over time and across contexts. Their previous stacking experiences provide a schema and a context for Kieran and Dylan to further their learning and to problem solve. The toddlers explore measurement and properties of shape, balance, and numeracy as they try to create a stack of clay cubes. They also explore physical science; they notice the cubes falling down due to the gravitational force, and they incorporate two different natural materials to create their towers. The simple combination of clay and wood allows the children to witness similarities and differences between these natural materials' textures and weights, and their different abilities to maintain balance and to hold their shape.

In addition, the toddlers are using their scientific and mathematical understandings to engage in engineering a tall, sturdy structure out of clay. Engineering and the creations of technology are a skill set applied to our current understandings of art, science, math, and social media. The children first start out with what they know: how to stack the cubes on top of each other, as they had done in their previous block play and other clay experiences. Kieran experiments with his hand techniques as he is very careful with his finger placements while stacking. He seems to have more of an engineering framework in place, evidenced by his creating a sturdy foundation of clay cubes, while Dylan is more playful with his initial stacking. Dylan is more interested in how high the clay cubes can stack easily and uses quick movements to place the clay cubes on top of each other.

Through the act of deconstruction, Dylan notices there are problems associated with his design; his tower has fallen multiple times. He searches elsewhere and outside of the confines of the clay activity before he finds a possible solution. This thinking is prompted by his final falling tower with Kieran, even after Kieran uses his own successful strategy from a previous stacking experience. Dylan looks to other resources and media available that might help support a similar stacking motion with the clay. He tries a new idea, that of retrieving cube-shaped wooden blocks, to further explore his tower-stacking problem. He uses the wood as another strategy and material for their shared stacking project. And it works! This experience further illustrates how children learn by their failures, challenges, and sticky moments when they are given time and resources to repeatedly explore natural dilemmas.

Learning happens in social contexts as do the science of technology and engineering. It was interesting to see how Dylan and Kieran notice each other's work. Slowly, and rather methodically, the toddlers come together to create a shared stacked tower. Often engineers need to pick out the best idea from a series of ideas for a given project. Dylan and Kieran have different thoughts and are able to integrate their ideas into a stronger, more grounded approach to their tower creations. In effect, they created a more reliable tower together than if they were doing it separately, as they had been doing in the beginning of the vignette.

Iris uses her feet and hands to get sensory feedback from the clay.

Iris begins to take ownership of her play with the clay block and adds small pieces to it. She engages in representation and labels the pieces of clay as buttons.

You can support children's engineering mind-set by keeping the learning platform moving and by being open to children's new discoveries. When Dylan and Kieran are making the stacked clay tower, their teacher is focusing more on keeping the two toddlers' experiences continuing than on providing the correct answer for Dylan and Kieran's balancing problem. Instead, the teacher gives them time to think and is open to Dylan's use of a different class material in their problem-solving journey. The teacher recognizes Dylan's big idea and expands on the idea, rather than limiting the way that the classroom materials are being used. Additionally, Dylan and Kieran's teacher has thought purposefully about the design and presentation of materials in their classroom; this thoughtful planning aids the toddlers' efforts in this given moment. Often it takes multiple experiences with multiple media before infants and toddlers can integrate their thinking across media simultaneously.

Future Possibilities and Reflections

The chapter describes how infants and toddlers can explore clay with their own unique interests. The clay adapts to the children's curiosities and imagination because of its transformative properties.

■ Amir is interested in how smaller pieces of clay could break off of the larger clay block. What types of experiences would Amir explore if there were a thinner clay slab for him to discover? The clay pieces might break off differently if the slab were thinner and therefore more likely to bend under the pressure of Amir's tiny fingers.

■ What other ways can clay be displayed for infants to explore when teachers are not present? Would they like to look at clay shapes being stored in airtight containers?

■ Dylan and Kieran have now integrated stacking clay and wood together to create towers. What other media might serve their interests with a larger scale? Would cardboard boxes and wood pieces serve a similar purpose for them?

■ How would Dylan and Kieran respond if they were given clay circles instead of clay cubes the next time they are introduced to a clay activity?

Chapter 3

STEAM Knowledge in Routines and Rituals

THIS CHAPTER SEEKS to illustrate how families' and caregivers' rituals and routines provide a deep and enriching STEAM learning environment for infants and toddlers. Vignettes depicting separations and reunions with family members further show how young children learn to use STEAM concepts in these social exchanges. Specific emphasis is placed on how very young children develop mathematical and art understandings through the exchanges that take place during reunions and separations. Ideas for how we can build learning from these ritual routines in the classroom are also explored.

Children's routines that are part of family and classroom practices provide optimal learning experiences because they are anticipated and repeated, and become very familiar. These practices can help reshape your perceptions about how and why children learn. Positive bonding experiences are formed between the children and the adults when teachers engage in routines. By establishing children's trusting relationships with others and materials, adults create environments that support children's inclination to take greater risks in engaging with STEAM concepts.

Presenting new media to infants and toddlers can provide intellectual and physical risks for children as they decide if it is safe to explore the new experiences. Children may wonder what they can do with the new material and how to explore it. Is it safe? Should I touch it? What can I do with this thing? Where are my caregivers or parents? These and many questions are pursued in children's first encounters with media.

Tobias, a three-month-old baby, explores a slab of clay with his parent for the first time. His father was unsure how his child would respond to the clay, and he used one of Tobias's blankets from home to provide familiarity to the new medium. Tobias and his father look and notice each other throughout this experience while responding to each other's cues. When Tobias was unsure, he was comforted by his father. They took the risk together because they trusted in each other and Tobias's family trusted in the process.

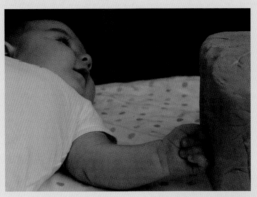

Tobias reaches for the clay and immediately holds his hands against the clay slab.

Tobias notices the difference in temperature between the clay and the hot day. He continues holding his fist against the clay for several minutes, indicating that he is interested in touching the new clay more.

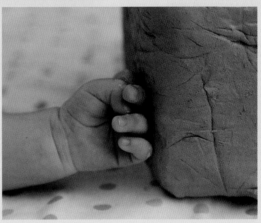

With time, recurring patterns become visible and children start to make routines themselves, all the while exploring the cause-and-effect relationships that happen with a given routine. Infants and toddlers may wonder what would happen if they changed a piece of their routine and waited for a response from the other engaged person. Rituals give meaning to why the routine is so important and the ways in which a specific routine is administered. Classroom and family ritual exchanges delicately support meaningful learning connected to children's families and classroom cultural norms related to STEAM concepts. Such recurring activities and regularities create a sustainable, manageable, and lasting means for children and their teachers to engage in development of STEAM concepts in partnership with families.

Saying Goodbye

Infants and toddlers are constantly reframing their thinking about given routines and ritual experiences. In the beginning, infants notice the sequences of the routines and start to anticipate what will happen next.

Sergei is an eleven-month-old infant who was born in Russia and came to the United States when he was six months old. He stays at home with his mother while his father works nearby. Sergei engages in goodbye routines with his father each morning. It is 9:00 a.m., and Sergei notices his father pick up a set of keys and a badge from the counter. Sergei quickly looks around to locate his shoes and hurries over toward them. He holds the shoes up high, indicating that he would like help with putting on his shoes. His mother sits down next to him, and Sergei promptly swings himself onto her lap. As his mother puts on Sergei's shoes, his father is putting on his shoes too.

Sergei's mother puts one shoe on each of his feet.

Sergei walks in front of his family to the apartment entry door. He taps on the door with his hands and arms while leaning his body up against it. His family responds with "Okay. Let's go." They open the door, and Sergei darts out in front of them, leading them in the right direction. He pauses to make sure that his family is following him before running ahead again. Sergei displays a sense of purpose and smiles each time he looks back to his parents, sometimes waiting for his parents to catch up. When he encounters a new turn, Sergei points to the direction that he plans to follow as an indication to his parents, *Go this way!*

Sergei slows down and stays closer to his mother as he approaches the final hallway exit door. His father walks ahead, and Sergei waves to him. Together the three of them have an intimate moment when Sergei waits with his mother while his father gets closer to the departure door. However, his father doesn't leave just yet, and Sergei quickly moves toward his dad. He falls down while walking and continues crawling without missing a beat. They give each other a hug, and then Sergei points to the door, similarly to how he indicated leaving the apartment. He moves over to the door and tries to push it open for his father, but the door doesn't move. He then goes back to his father and points in the door's direction a final time before giving his father one last hug. They say goodbye and separate. Sergei turns around and walks back to his mother for a hug. They head back to their apartment.

On the way back, Sergei walks more slowly. He stops at all of his favorite places, including the neighbors' apartment doormats and other hallway features. Sergei knows where the indoor rock garden is and picks up some of the rocks before indicating that he is ready to go back inside his own apartment. He looks up to his mother and smiles when he notices something different or in a new location in the hallway.

Sergei indicated that he is beginning to understand a sense of direction and time. Each of these concepts are quantifiable measurements used in many STEAM concept environments. He understood the correct direction that his father took every day to go to work and remembered where specific objects were located along the way. He found his way through a series of mazelike hallways that led him around the apartment units, showing a deep understanding of space. Sergei noticed how long something would take and when certain events took place throughout his day, indicating a notion of time and the relationships of events in time.

Sergei created rituals for these routines by establishing ways of interacting with the information that he was continuously processing. For example, Sergei was carefully calculating how many people were with him before determining to move ahead and run forward. He looked to see that his mother and father were together, a mathematical concept that involves parts-to-whole relationships. This number understanding was also evident in the way Sergei looked for his shoes; he found two shoes and then held them up in the air to indicate that he was ready to go. Notice that his family placed one shoe on each of his feet and followed his cues within their given goodbye routine sequences. The ways that his family responded to Sergei's bids for interaction further reinforced his understandings of STEAM concepts.

Sergei used his STEAM concept knowledge to make sense of his separation from his father. Naturally, Sergei was able to make predictions based on space, object locations, and his relationships with his family. He actively investigated cause and effect with how he took a turn or led his family to say goodbye. He tried different strategies to test his predictions in the goodbye routine and seemed to stop to gain feedback about these strategies. He seemed to retain a memory of where he was in space while walking to the "goodbye" door. He carefully sequenced his routines and broke down the routines into smaller parts. He knew that as he neared that final hallway bend, he would then be saying goodbye. This spatial and distance awareness allowed him to identify when the ending of his goodbye routine would occur. As a result, he could predict and be ready for the goodbye as it happened. In these intimate exchanges, Sergei felt safe to take greater risks in his own thinking and movements.

Sergei waits by the door his father will eventually go through on his way to work.

Sergei engages in art media in the STEAM concepts by actively designing how he facilitates saying goodbye to his father. The way he expresses his thoughts through body movement and facial expressions indicates his understanding of specific STEAM concepts. With each directional change, Sergei adjusts his movements to point into the new to-be-traveled space. Sergei modifies his design with each reiteration of saying goodbye. He notices what types of communication work better with his family, and he skillfully uses this information in his goodbye exchange. For Sergei, who is still learning how to say words, using his body's expression and gestures turns out to be the best design for sharing his ideas and goodbyes in the goodbye routine. He expresses many sounds and gestures to communicate his ideas and creates an urgency for his requests. This artful expression helps his family understand what he wants to communicate and to be more attuned to Sergei's future discoveries of STEAM concepts. The family's feedback is driven by the moment-to-moment exchanges. Rituals are established in how the family communicates different concepts to each other in their goodbye routine. Consequently, Sergei's family extends and expands on his thinking, and their ideas emerge as a result of his artful expression.

Saying Hello: Building Routines to Reunite with Families

In this vignette, the teachers have carefully constructed a goodbye circle with the families to facilitate the infants' and toddlers' departures from school. We see how the teachers and parents use visuals, systems, and children's interests to highlight STEAM concepts with the children's reunion routines.

It is four thirty in the afternoon, and the children are getting ready for their parents to take them home after a long day at school. Teachers share with the infants and toddlers that it is gathering time. They invite the children to join them if they would like, and all the teachers sit together. They place carpet squares on the floor for the children to sit on. Some of the infants, who have just started walking, are reaching out to hold their carpet squares on their laps, while other older toddlers jump onto the squares nearby. Teachers hold very young infants in their laps, and everyone gathers around the meeting space.

Once everyone is settled, visual systems are utilized to engage the infants and toddlers in the goodbye ritual. One teacher presents sound cards with pictures on them that represent a song. The teacher holds the cards in front for the infants and toddlers so they can each pick a song. Some of the children search for their favorite songs, while others want to have more than one card. Each infant and toddler is given a turn to present a card to the group, and then everyone sings the song associated with the card. One of the infants holds her card outward, indicating that she is ready to sing her chosen song. The teacher shares with the group that Iris wants to sing her song now. They sing "Twinkle, Twinkle, Little Star" together, and Iris smiles. After a few songs are sung, the teacher takes out her ukulele. This excites Dylan, and he quickly reaches toward the ukulele. The teacher invites him to play the song with her while the other children sing the next child's song. Dylan strums the ukulele with his fingers and puts the ukulele on his lap. The teacher supports his efforts, and he goes back to his space once the song is over.

The children are gathered around their teachers singing a song when the families arrive.

Families trickle in while the children sing songs together. One parent quietly sits down on the couch, smiling at his son until the song has ended. The completion of the song prompts the child to giggle and move closer to his father. They join each other with warm contact, and the father picks up Ollie and sets him on his lap for the next song. They enjoy the music for a few more minutes, and then the father stands up and goes to read Ollie's daily charts, which are located away from their gathering space. Ollie remains with his peers for another song. Suddenly, Ollie wants to be near his parent, and he runs toward his father, who is standing by his cubby nearby. They embrace each other one more time, and his father lifts Ollie up close to his chest. They gather their things and walk to the door. The children notice that Ollie is leaving, and they sing a special goodbye song to the departing family.

Ollie gets up after the
song finishes and moves
toward his parent.

Teachers intentionally facilitated the reunion gathering to fit the children's social
needs and cognitive development. Some of these activities engaged the children in
learning more about STEAM concepts. The teacher asked the child, "Do you want
two songs today?" She waited for the child to answer and provided more than one
option for the child to choose from. This exchange not only validated the child's
choice, but it also pointed out concepts of quantity and numeracy for the infant. The
child identified that two was more than one and tangibly held two cards in hand for
the activity. Two songs were sung in addition to holding the two cards. This refined
understanding of what the number two means can later be replicated by children
with more iterations of the routine. The children may begin to notice how many
cards are shared in total with the whole group. They recognize how many cards other
children are holding.

As we sing the songs, it becomes apparent that the songs have a purpose too. Many of the songs involve moving one's body up and down, fast and slow, among many other directional or quantifiable factors. The songs have beginnings and endings for the children to discover. Some of the songs focus on inventions like trains, cars, and other fascinating topics for children. They begin to see how sound is produced with the ukulele and see the instrument as a tool, a concept that the teacher allows the children to actively engage in by handing over the instrument for the children to try.

Additionally, the children recognize how their own family reunion routines connect with their daily classroom experiences. Some of the children expect their parent to come near them, while others go to their cubbies to get ready to leave. The very young children are beginning to see how their ideas are related to other people's thoughts. A series of routines at school provides a sense of time for the children to discover and to engage in. During Ollie's parental reunion, Ollie clearly waited for the ending of a song before he chose to sit next to his parent. He listened to the different rhythms and lyrics of the music so he would know when the end of the song was going to happen. Ollie knew that there were multiple parts to his going-home routine and waited for his parent to be ready before leaving the gathering space. They concluded this goodbye routine with a goodbye song from his peers.

Ollie and Dylan pick their choice cards from their teacher.

Establishing STEAM Concept Learning through Current Routines and Rituals

You have a tremendous opportunity to engage infants and toddlers with STEAM concepts while going through very young children's daily routines and rituals in the classroom. Infants and toddlers have many needs that are routinely addressed throughout their day—for example, diaper changing, sleeping, and eating. Through intentional interactions and supports focused on children's routines and rituals, you can encourage children to think more deeply. Once children become comfortable with a given routine or ritual exchange, they are more likely to acquire additional skills. Infants, toddlers, and adults can uncover new sources of knowledge by incorporating small next steps into their already established routines. Often next steps happen spontaneously and naturally in the routine when the children or adults try out something new.

Infants and toddlers who have established familiarity with routines can revisit them, adding greater complexity and reflection. Deeply established routines and rituals provide space for young children to make predictions about what will happen next. They start to remember what happened the last time in the routine and who was involved. Familiarity with routines and rituals allows infants and toddlers to engage in more process-oriented activities. The children have some familiar routine platforms to branch off from and to consider how something evolves, grows, or creates new form. In STEAM learning, establishing routines related to science media or other technological tools can further children's understandings of STEAM concepts.

The established routines or rituals used with materials can be transferred to other science media and technology tools. In this effort, the children spend less time

Kianna and Nola role-play the end-of-day gathering that they participate in each afternoon with their classmates.

accessing STEAM learning material and more on the actual activity itself. Young children learn a great deal when they are encouraged to replicate their commonly held routines in their play, as in the photo on page 36. The children set up the routine by sitting on chairs together. They role-play the different adult roles in the routine; they are exploring the different perspectives to the given routine. They sing songs that they remember are sung during the routine as well. Over time, teachers could present new songs or add more steps to the routine for the infants and toddlers to experience. The children are gaining mastery of their skills with each iteration of their routines both in play and in classroom practices. Children have the same tools, space, and activity to engage with, but they have a slight change in the medium. As we can see, the rituals involved in how the routine is administered remain the same so that the child can explore different STEAM concepts with each routine attempt.

The intention of the different types of activities to which children are exposed and the "why" often resonate in classroom or home rituals and routines. Consider what your overarching goal is with each given routine, and break it down into small steps. Once you have identified the different interactions established in a simple routine, try to connect each of these interactions to a particular STEAM learning stance. This will allow you to be focused on each part of the routine as you engage in the whole STEAM learning process.

Future Possibilities and Reflections

It is clear that routines evolve with time and the children's needs. The routines engage children with STEAM concepts and provide support for young children as they wait for their families to come back. It can be hard for a child to see another family leave and to wait longer for her own family to arrive. Therefore, the routine promotes a healthier reunion for all the children at this tricky time of the day. Knowing the benefits of the routine helps teachers identify how they can continue the STEAM concept learning in the routine experience.

- What would it look like to introduce different STEAM concept songs in the choice song cards repertoire?

- In what ways could the teachers connect their efforts to the production of sound and an instrument's technology?

- Using different colored squares or shaped carpet spaces, how could teachers highlight colors and patterns in some of the songs they sing together?

- Could the children create their own sound cards or introduce new songs from home?

Chapter 4

Engaging in STEAM Concepts with Multipurpose Materials

THE JOURNEYS that infants and toddlers embark on while collecting fascinating and beautiful objects can captivate them and uncover new STEAM learning concepts. Classification is a basic cognitive structure that humans use to understand the world. Collecting objects provides multiple opportunities for classifying: by shape, by color, by size, by use, and so forth. Shared collections allow children to express themselves and to discover new bits of information in playful collective experiences. Culture, knowledge, and current technologies directly influence the types of methods people use to store and access their collections. People practice different methodologies to preserve foods, store liquids, and organize an abundance of materials and data. Observing how other people collect materials can provide valuable information about what people know about their collections and why they are pursuing them.

Very young children are curious learners who spend great lengths of time collecting materials in play. Infants and toddlers want to hold, accumulate, and share their materials with others. Often they seek out random, repurposed, or transportable materials around them to interact with and use. Children notice how their peers use the materials and later replicate what they have observed in their current play experiences. Activities that have a natural appeal for very young children include putting materials in and out of holes, exploring the moving parts of containers, and spatially interacting with three-dimensional objects.

In this series of photos, Chelsea constructs with tubes and cones, displaying a desire to balance and connect the two cones to a nearby tube.

Experiencing Technology: How Objects Open and Close

Infants and toddlers explore a multitude of similar tags with loose parts and repurposed containers in the following vignettes. The children bring their own thoughts and understandings to the playful experience. The teachers observe the children's present ideas around the objects at hand and provide extensions to the children's learning when needed. The infants and toddlers investigate a common theme: how objects go in and out. We examine how infants and young toddlers approach tools to collect their play materials.

Zoe, an eleven-month-old infant, interacts with the tags and nearby containers first by observing and then by trying out activities with them. She watches her friends pick up the containers nearby and witnesses the containers being used as tools for collection. The children are storing their materials inside the containers. A teacher notices Zoe's gaze as she visually follows her peers around the room. Recognizing Zoe's interest, the teacher brings over a container with a lid for Zoe to tinker with. She opens the container for Zoe to discover what is inside. Zoe touches the green paper tags inside the container with her fingertips. She picks up one of the green tags and brings it to her mouth. While sucking on the paper, Zoe observes again how her friends are using the lids and containers. Her peers are moving the tags into the plastic jars until each jar is completely full, sealing the collection with the container's lid afterward.

Zoe's interest takes a turn as she tries to fasten the lid onto her container. She reaches for the plastic container's sides to pick the whole thing up. After some time, Zoe tries to put the lid on top of the container. She doesn't succeed right away. Zoe looks at her container and then observes her peers' interactions. With each of her attempts to attach the lid to her container, she is noticing the sequence of events that need to take place. Simultaneously, this sequence is being modeled by her peers when they tighten and loosen the lids on their similar containers nearby. Zoe is inspired to try their modeled method. She picks up the white lid and places it onto the clear container with one hand. This time she has the correct side facing down for the screwing motion to work with the container. The lid rests on top of her container but could easily fall off if bumped. For Zoe, this is the beginning of her journey to discover how she could utilize the container in the future. With time and dexterity, she will be able to screw the lid onto the base.

Zoe attempts to put the lid onto the top of the jar.

Zoe pursues a strategy that works for her to set the lid on the jar.

Zoe interacts with engineering concepts in her attempt to place the lid onto the container. She establishes which of the object's properties can be modified and which properties remain stable. For example, Zoe observes and discovers that the lid will not change its shape to better fit the container. Rather, she needs to adjust how she uses the lid to properly attach it to the container. Toward the end of her experience, Zoe has an aha moment when she discovers the correct handgrip and finger placement for her to properly place the lid facing down on the container. This discovery displays how Zoe uses her scientific and technological understandings to find solutions for connecting the container's lid with its base.

Now that we witnessed how Zoe interacts with the container, let's take a deeper look at how Amir encounters opening and closing a plastic fruit carton with multiple moving parts. He starts to manipulate the flaps of the containers before he displays an interest in the collection of materials. Amir notices that the container has movable parts and tries to reproduce these movements repeatedly. He pushes on top of the container, causing the plastic clamshell carton to move with each attempt. The container closes with one of his forceful pushes and does not open again. The plastic fruit carton has a small opening between the lid and the container's base. Amir revises his thinking and comes up with a new idea.

Amir tinkers with the plastic clam-shaped container.

Amir stands up on his feet and pushes the container together. It springs open when he lets go.

Amir tries a different strategy to open and close the container while standing.

He begins to pry open this small space with his finger instead of using his previous method of pushing down from the top. The new approach allows Amir to move the container's lid easily, and it is altogether more responsive to Amir's small finger movements. And then the container springs open!

Amir looks up with a smile, and his teacher points out that the container is now open. The teacher wonders what he is going to do next. Amir recently expanded his mobility by learning how to stand. This new mobility prompts him to consider how to close the container with different body positions. Amir tries to manipulate the container in yet another manner: bending and standing. He stands up on his feet and carefully tries to close the container by using his large motor movements as he pushes the plastic container against his stomach.

In this exchange, Amir accesses the art and engineering concepts in STEAM learning by problem solving with an engineering mind-set. He uses the art medium of design to find out ways to open and close the plastic fruit container. Similar to Zoe, he first discovers the current functionalities that the lid and container technologies provide. He notices that the lid can be moved and possibly opened or closed by his peers. He tries to figure out how he can move the container by himself. Then he uses a variety of designs to test out ways to open and close the container by adjusting the space, the ways he moves his body, and his body position with each attempt. The design offers different feedback for Amir that he later takes and organizes together. Amir is putting pieces of a puzzle together in each design attempt to better understand how the object can open and close. In the end, Amir has a more solid understanding of the fruit carton and its functionality because he repeats opening and closing it from so many different angles.

Both Amir and Zoe are interested in figuring out how containers function and work in their play. They access many STEAM learning concepts in their learning journeys and question some of their ideas through active explorations. Careful observations of children pursuing questions, interests, and concepts can give us greater understanding of how we can continue our STEAM learning journeys with them.

As we reflect on what Amir and Zoe are telling us in their play experiences, we can look at the role that the environment has for young children in their learning. They are always looking toward what objects can be manipulated and in what ways. We notice how an object's moving parts can motivate children's deeper explorations of how an object functions. Infants and toddlers invest and persevere through a series of learning events to accomplish their set-out goals. The environment seems big to young children, and often they notice similarities between one learning experience and other lived moments. In Zoe's STEAM learning, she was watching how the environment was being used in addition to how she could tangibly move objects in space. She may notice these same movements in a different context when she witnesses her family prepare meals and open containers similar to the one that she previously investigated at school. We can never know everything that infants are thinking about, but we can try to know by carefully observing how the children are building their understandings with their connections to their environments.

As we noted in chapter 1, children are the problem posers. They find out what kinds of situations they can create with objects to further explore their thinking. In Amir's example, he uses his new mobility to create new problems for opening and closing the container as he manipulates the container in the air while standing, bending, and sitting. When we understand the patterns that children are investigating, then we, as teachers, can set up new extensions to the children's learning or propose new problems for the children to discover. We could provide different moving objects that follow or contradict Amir's current thinking. We could set up moving objects that close like a clamshell for Amir to continue to explore, or we could present new moving objects that function differently than a clam-shaped container. One method provides a space for the child to master their ideas and STEAM concepts, while the other method gives space for new discoveries to be made with STEAM learning.

Integrating Mathematics and Science with Materials

Children are scientists. We see children's scientific literacy demonstrated when they explore the properties of basic materials. Infants and toddlers continually try to find a material's limits. Children seek out what objects can be bent and which ones will break easily with not too much bending. They notice how materials can stay in fluid or solid states. They discover whether an object can provide support to another object when stacking two objects together. All of these observations share a little bit more about the object's scientific properties and its possibilities for use as a tool in our society.

Ollie investigates how to put a yellow tag into a cardboard tube.

Ollie experiences categorization when material is presented in color categories.

Ollie attempts again to put the yellow tags back into a cardboard circular opening with the cardboard cone.

As children learn more about some materials' properties, they creatively interact with the materials while applying a solution-centered approach. They start to find solutions to how they can use different materials in their daily play dilemmas. They access their previous scientific knowledge to create new tools for their play, especially if a former known tool is not available. The engineer mind tries to think of the easiest and simplest way to solve the problem with the provided tools, materials, and knowledge. We witnessed this take place in the ways that the children stored, sorted, collected, or utilized the materials.

Throughout the collection of materials, children are finding ways to quantify how much or how many group items they currently have. Infants and toddlers may determine quantity when they cannot fit more into a container or when they see the materials spread out across the floor. With each repetitive collection, they begin to notice differences in quantity and size from a new perspective. They start to measure how much something is by using a similar unit of measurement, like a cup, bowl, or purse. Some children may want to explore only the "act of measuring" over and over, while others want to measure once and keep their collected items for the whole day.

Carlos explores measuring with a cup container while playing in the sand. His consistent interactions with the cup and other media provide greater understanding with regard to quantity and space.

Toddlers Exploring Space and Quantity

Toddlers are drawn to interact with and transport objects in their play. We see this when toddlers collect objects and store them in a nearby purse, pocket, or lap space. They are constantly trying to access their collected objects from different angles and with tangible strategies. Sometimes toddlers incorporate their own assertive ideas and hypotheses with other peers and adults nearby. They use their thinking about and active explorations of objects to further discover the object's known purposes. In this vignette, we will illustrate how toddlers collect objects and transport them through space. We seek to distinguish the STEAM concept learning that emerges from toddlers' daily activities with collecting open-ended materials. We will high-light toddlers' problem solving and symbolic thinking in their play as they explore space, dimension, and scale with the collected objects.

As Iris explores the tags, she begins to experiment with what pieces will fit into different sized containers. Iris transports the yellow tags from her wicker basket to a clear plastic container. She is faced with the challenge of collecting all the yellow plastic tags in the smaller, clear container. This container presents itself differently from her previous basket container, which fit all of the pieces at once. The yellow tags are sticking out of the plastic container, and Iris is unable to screw the lid on as a result. Consequently, Iris takes a few yellow tags out of the plastic container and tries again. The yellow plastic corners of the tags

Iris transfers yellow tags from the basket into the clear, plastic container.

still protrude from the container's rim, and Iris has no luck screwing the lid back onto the container. After some time, she places all the yellow tags back into her basket and drives the basket around in an even larger wooden cart on wheels.

This wicker basket easily holds all of the yellow tags that Iris was collecting.

As the children explore how they can collect many materials in a given space, some concepts arise related to geometry, numeracy, and measurement. They notice which objects fit better into the containers and use these underlying understandings in their play. For example, Iris stops her efforts to fit the objects into the smaller container and then finds a larger wheeled container to broaden her play with the materials. Children are constantly problem solving how they can manipulate materials, combine and separate materials, and measure materials within a given space. These experiences provide a way for them to explore the object's dimensions in connection to the available volume of a given space.

Iris expands on her mathematical concepts of space by not forcing the objects into her plastic container but instead using a new, larger container to transport the materials around the yard. She measures the set space in the smaller container and determines that she had "too much" for that given area. The container serves as a tool to quantify and measure the amount of space needed for her set number of yellow tags that she is collecting. This tool use highlights how children naturally find ways to engage with technology in play and are driven to accomplish their determined goals with these tool resources.

Iris transports the basket of tags in her cart until she finds a spot to sit down and look at them again.

Iris's friend Dylan explores the yellow tags with a geometric twist. Dylan is curious to see how their sides and corners can fit as a grouped unit into a container system. He starts out by placing a few tags together to form a larger shape. Then he picks up this larger shape with his hands and places it into his containers. Noticing a clear slotted container nearby, Dylan carefully picks up three more yellow tags at the same time and then places the larger shape on its side to fit into the desired slot. The slot container has different affordances for Dylan to explore with the materials, and he is inspired to think about how shapes can be created when combined.

After exploring this idea, Dylan has a new thought. He notices that he can stack the larger containers to create a bigger structure. He places one clear pink tag container under the yellow tag one. He reaches for a blue tag container and positions that container on the very top. Each container is specific and has its own color of tag inside. If a different-color tag is inside, Dylan takes it out and places it into its color's container. After counting the three stacked-up containers, Dylan starts to deconstruct them again. He wants to re-create the process.

Dylan puts the yellow tags into the clear plastic slots.

Dylan stacks and categorizes the tags with their three containers.

Dylan acquires more knowledge about scalability with each stacking iteration and collection of tags. He gains more understanding about how to determine how much something is when he systematically organizes objects together in smaller to larger quantities. Dylan starts out by exploring how a few tags can be combined together to form a basic grouping and then later collects the different-colored tags into multiple larger groupings of blue, yellow, and pink tags. He is beginning to understand how many parts there are in the displayed group of objects when he categorizes the tags into separate-colored containers. He uses scale to measure how big the objects are by examining one container independently and then relates this experience to a larger one by placing three similar-shaped containers on top of each other. In essence, Dylan is learning more about how objects with similar units can be added or removed from a set quantity. Moreover, scalability allows Dylan to better identify the capacity for these pieces to be quantified, similar to how scientists discuss scale systems to measure our existence in the vast universe or our ecosystems. Dylan sees how one container influences the other containers and explores this cause-and-effect relationship with his future ideas.

Later that afternoon, Dylan transports his collection to a new play setting and manipulates the same materials in his play. He picks up one container filled with yellow tags and takes it to a garbage truck in the sand. Dylan begins taking out the yellow tags and placing them into the garbage truck. His friend Ollie comes over and does the same activity. The two children place all the tags they can find into the garbage trucks. The design of the garbage truck lid helps hold these tags inside the truck. Ollie and Dylan move quickly, pushing their garbage trucks in front of them as they give their tags a ride around the yard. It seems that the tags have turned into symbols of garbage. All of a sudden, the tags fall out of the garbage truck and spread across the sand. Ollie stops to look at all the objects and stares at the ground. Dylan comes over and looks too. Ollie remarks, "So big!" Together the two children collect the material off the sand and continue their garbage-truck play.

Dylan unscrews the container with yellow tags to place the tags into the garbage truck.

The tags fit inside the garbage truck, and the truck's lid design keeps the tags inside.

Throughout this experience, the children explore how one particular geometric shape can fit inside the space of a different geometric shape. Ollie and Dylan find ways to put the yellow rectangular tags inside the garbage truck. The design of the garbage truck provides different affordances for the children to transport the materials, displaying another level of how children engage in moving objects through space. At one point, Ollie and Dylan are overwhelmed with how many yellow tags they have when the objects are spread across the sand. Notice that they did not have the same feelings when the same number of objects was being stored in their confined garbage truck spaces. It seems that they feel the yellow objects take up more space when spread out on the ground in comparison to when the objects are stored inside the garbage trucks. This is a common thought that infants and toddlers hold while exploring numeracy and quantity; they may think that more means how big or how much space the object takes in comparison to the actual number the group of objects represent (Piaget and Inhelder 1974).

Ollie transports his items around in the garbage truck.

Play provides a wonderful opportunity for children to explore STEAM concepts because in play children have a space for testing and exploring new and revisited ideas through improvisation. In this experience, the children first find out what the underlying capabilities of the yellow tags are before they incorporate them into their symbolic play. Naturally, they want to know how they can access the materials before engaging the materials in their play with each other. Play also lets children try new concepts and learn by observing another child's ideas. We see this happen with Ollie and Dylan as they spontaneously build a story around collecting yellow tags with their garbage trucks. Ollie notices Dylan's play and replicates a similar idea in his own associative play with Dylan.

The tags spill out onto the sandy floor. Ollie and Dylan notice how many tags are on the ground.

Future Possibilities and Reflections

Creating extensions to infants' and toddlers' STEAM learning is a creative process. It requires us to think beyond what we already know. Below are some possible venues that you might consider in providing future extensions to the children.

- What other slot-like containers could the children explore with these materials? It would be interesting to have these slotted materials placed on vertical and horizontal planes for the children to assess.

- What would it look like if the abundance of materials were a different geometric shape from a square? Would the children have similar experiences if the materials were round like balls?

- What kinds of technology or real-life experiences could the children access to better inform their playful exchanges with the garbage trucks and tags?

- How could the children explore force and gravity in these experiences? Would it be beneficial to set up some ramps or platforms for the trucks to drive on?

Chapter 5

STEAM in Movement and Music

M OVEMENT PROVIDES OPPORTUNITIES to explore natural STEAM concepts and further define our capacities as human beings. The way we move in space can give us information about our place in the world. We are continually connected to the space around us, and our movements in space inspire us to discover new possibilities. We may notice the different pitches that occur on the guitar based on where and how we strum the instrument's strings. On a larger scale, astronauts' adventures to great unknown spaces outside of Earth's atmosphere introduced movement experiences without a strong gravitational force. In a smaller space, we explore finer body movements to draw and design blueprints of thinking not yet attempted. Movement allows us to see the world and to make connections within it.

Children's movements provide new chapters and milestones for STEAM concept discoveries. Many STEAM concepts can be understood through children's basic movements. Infants and toddlers communicate with their movements as they sign words, move toward things they desire, and create sounds with objects. They are learning how to stand, balance, roll, sit, run, walk, jump, go over, go under, and perform other movements in their typical motor development. With each iteration of movement, children find out more about how much force is needed to physically move their bodies. They experience how far their steps can take them and observe depth from different perspectives while standing, jumping, climbing, and crawling. These movements themselves tell us much about speed, directionality, measurability, and geometry. For example, an infant can use speed to access items in the classroom before being picked up by an adult to go outside. When they interact with objects in their environments, infants and toddlers begin to understand physically how things balance and move.

Infants' and toddlers' movements provide a platform for understanding motion. *Motion* is defined as the process or action of moving. As we discussed in the beginning of the book, children learn through their physical knowledge experiences with objects around them (Kamii and DeVries 1993). Very young children translate their physical movement experiences onto the movements and manipulation of objects. As infants learn to control their arm movements, they are better equipped to witness how a material will fall after releasing it. They see how balls roll farther based on how fast they move their arms while letting go. Infants and toddlers are building pathways to understanding cause and effect each time they observe their movement's impact on objects. They begin to use movements for sound production as they connect, hit, or slide objects together. They identify traces of their own motions as they move their bodies across sand or writing materials across paper.

Taking Risks: Moving through Space

Children use their STEAM concept understanding to cognitively determine what next steps they need to make when problem solving a new experience. The following vignette illustrates one child's first attempt to ride a bike and highlights the different STEAM concepts the child accessed in this experience. Mathematical concepts further articulate how the twelve-month-old uses space, science, and technology to create a motor plan for sequencing her bodily movements with the bike.

> Zoe displays an interest in joining her classmates through movement as she uses her body to ride a bike. She communicates her ideas with a pointing gesture to her teacher nearby. Zoe points in the direction of the stored bikes and begins to crawl out of the sand toward the bikes. As she gets closer to the counter where the bikes are stored, she says, "Ba, ba, ba." The nearby teacher hears Zoe's requests and goes to her. Zoe continues to point to the bikes while repeating, "Ba, ba, ba." By this time, the teacher understands Zoe's interest and takes down a bike from the counter so that Zoe can access it. The teacher asks Zoe, "Do you want to go on the bike?" Zoe continues to look at the bike and touches the handlebars. Her teacher picks her up and sets her on the bike seat.
>
> Zoe, who just started walking, begins to coordinate her movements to use the space around the bike to make it move. Zoe stretches her legs out so that her feet touch the ground on both sides. Her hands are on the

handlebars, similar to her peers, who are moving their bikes past her. With time, Zoe starts to rock her body back and forth. She moves her upper body forward and brings it back to an upright position. She notices that the bike moves. Zoe rocks harder and the bike inches forward even more. She continues until she is able to move the bike one bike length. Then she stops. She sticks out her tongue in concentration and lets go of the handlebars.

After some time, Zoe indicates that she is done riding the bike and wants help getting off. She starts to move her leg over the bike seat so she can dismount. Feeling a bit wobbly, Zoe brings her foot back to its original position. The teacher reaches out her arm, and Zoe easily accepts it. While holding on to the teacher's hand, Zoe shifts her weight to one side and lifts her leg up to get off the bike. The teacher provides Zoe space to coordinate her movements while still holding on to the bike's frame so that it doesn't roll away. Zoe gets up on her tippy toes and successfully moves her leg over the bike and onto the ground. She did it! Holding the handlebars still, Zoe lets go of the teacher's hand and points to the bike seat. We wonder what she is telling us after getting off the bike for the first time.

Zoe's peers ride the bikes around her outside.

Zoe points to the bikes and crawls toward them.

Zoe's teacher places her onto the bike.

Zoe balances on the bike. She tries to make it move.

Zoe tries to move her leg over the bike seat.

Zoe remains in her original position. She is unsure how she will get off the bike.

Zoe takes her teacher's hands to get off the bike.

Zoe stands on her tippy toes and moves her weight over to one side.

The teacher steadies the bike for her.

Zoe finds her way back to the floor next to the bike.

Zoe points to the bike seat where she was just sitting.

Zoe explores the intersections of STEAM concepts about movement when she uses the bike in her play. In this bike experimentation, Zoe is learning more about force, wheels as a tool, and distance being traveled. She could be remembering how toy cars move from her past play experiences, or maybe she is remembering past observations of her peers riding their bikes around her. She doesn't know how to make the bike move yet because she hasn't tried it before, but she has a general understanding of what could happen if she did try. And then she tries it.

With each rocking motion, Zoe experiences the speed in her movements while on the bike. She notices the cause-and-effect relationship associated with her rocking movements and the distance the bike travels. When she uses faster movements, the bike responds more. She begins to measure her speed and applies force to her movements by replicating fast rocking motions. Her bike moves farther. Zoe might not be able to tease out the difference between speed and force, but she is immersing herself in this whole-body experience to find out more about it. Zoe is defining how movements are connected to objects being transferred through space.

More tangibly, Zoe figures out how to move herself around the bike's geometric shape through a series of experiments. She explores cause and effect with her body-movement experiments. Notice how she starts to rock her body to make the bike move after she has tried other movement attempts (placing her feet on the ground, touching the handlebars, and moving her leg over and back again from the seat position). In one of her experimental movements, Zoe feels unbalanced and brings her leg back to its original position. She retrieves previously obtained information to design an experiment to get off of the bike. The simple act of moving her leg over and down the bike requires her to visually plan out her movements so she can get to a desired position off of the bike. These movement plans access Zoe's geometric understandings of the bike in connection to her bodily awareness in space. She becomes familiar with how high her leg can stretch and is mentally calculating if she can reach the point in space for her leg to reach the ground. Then she accommodates this newly obtained piece of information to design a different way to get off the bike. She requests help from a teacher, uses her tippy toes for more leverage, and shifts her weight differently with her next attempt.

Zoe is using the moment-to-moment feedback from her movements and relating this information to what she knows will happen when she physically moves objects around in the world. She is using what she learned from riding the bike and relates this experience to STEAM concept understandings. She is comparing what is happening with what she already knows. Her pointing to the seat after getting off the bike further indicates that she is reflecting on what she did. This small gesture points out that Zoe can visualize herself being on the seat from her past experiences. We don't always think of toddlers as being reflective, but this example shows they can be. Because she is reflecting back, she is creating a more complicated experience.

In this new milestone experience, Zoe also learns more about how wheels function and move. She applies what she currently knows about movement to this new bike experience. She knows that wheels can travel across space and that pushing something will make it move. Likewise, the bike is a tool for children to move around their space quickly and efficiently. In this situation, Zoe gains a deeper understanding of how wheels move and how the bike can serve her own purposes. Zoe figures out ways to control the tool before she uses it for a more defined purpose in play. She coordinates her movements to move the bike. Zoe's investigation with the bike identifies what her body could do in space with an added tool. Many of Zoe's movements are intertwined and connect to her past experiences. She associates her balancing steps from walking with the movements required for her to balance on the bike seat. Zoe discovers another way to use her physical movements to manipulate technology.

Thinking about what children already know before introducing a new STEAM concept allows us to better plan curriculum to facilitate the children's access to the materials and point them toward the possible places the learning will take them. When you connect the common threads of what the children are already doing to a new planned experience, you can deepen the children's relationship with the STEAM concept. In Zoe's experience, learning how to get on the bike herself would have helped her figure out how to get off the bike. Many times children remember some of the steps to get on the bike and will use this previous knowledge to figure out the reverse steps to get off the bike.

Soundscapes and Engineering

Infants' and toddlers' disposition to discover their worlds naturally engages them in engineering sound-producing experiences. Children access sound by manipulating their environments and creating new sound experiences. They are like little engineers going around their environments, picking up sticks, buckets, metal objects, and more to use as tools to learn more about a given concept. They begin to notice which tools work best for specific sounds and the kinds of sounds they can make. We see this when children close doors loudly or use ladles to bang against pans.

How we talk about sound production and the ways that we model, promote, and use sound can have a profound impact on the different types of STEAM concepts children experience. We may want to introduce a musical instrument as a tool for people to make sounds and then share how the children have been making their own sounds. The classroom can provide other materials for children to explore sound if the musical instruments are out of reach. Infants, even three to four months of age, create different tempos and sounds when given the chance to move nearby rings attached to sound mobiles above them. Teachers can give the sounds names, as many children like to have words to associate with objects and experiences. Finding ways for young children to create loud sounds further articulates for the children the different volumes and tones associated with their sound productions.

An instrument has so much to offer to children besides the sound production itself. When we let children explore the different components of instruments, we are giving children the opportunity to manipulate the sound as well as to create sound. Often an instrument is composed of many pieces and may require sequenced steps to put it together. Many components connected to the instrument further alter the sound production. Noticing how each piece changes the sounds can be fascinating for young children and further depicts how sound can be manipulated. As children get older, we find our language and interactions with instruments become more complex. Toddlers may use instruments to portray symbolic representations of different feelings and situations. The ways that they design their sounds to represent specific patterns becomes a common language for all the children to connect with. The sound begins to represent meaning to their peers and teachers. We all can remember the fast drumming of a child who is feeling excited.

Dylan manipulates his teacher's ukulele during a music gathering. His peers do the same, and they begin to notice the different types of sounds they can create with the ukulele's strings.

Children can create their own sounds out of available materials. Pipes and tunnels can be a provocation to enhance children's humming and sound productions in their play.

Defining how and where sound can be manipulated is something that infants and toddlers explore in their play. Professional sound engineers use an understanding in their work similar to what very young children use in their play environments. The different acoustics and mixing of sounds are created in the environments. You may notice infants and toddlers exploring an echo, a particular type of sound, or a space that amplifies their sound's volume. As they become preschoolers, the children may begin to wonder how sound can invisibly travel through space and try to illustrate their soundscapes in their drawings. Even though young children do not know how to articulate what they are refining, like a sound engineer does in their workplace, they are paying close attention to these finer details associated with sound.

Creating Music with Movements

Music and movement serve as connecting media for adults to observe children's STEAM learning and for young children to investigate STEAM concepts. Children find ways to articulate and express newly acquired STEAM concepts to their peers through the exploration of art media found in music and performance. We will explore how a toddler examines pitch and the production of sound by engaging in a drumming experience. The investigation of sound continues when the child utilizes a mallet to better articulate sound production with different parts of a drum. We conclude the vignette by discussing how movements are related to sound traveling through space.

The children begin to gather around the drums to sing songs and make music. All of the children but Ollie are nearby. Ollie is out finding bugs in the playground. Ollie seems less interested in the drumming sounds but becomes very excited when he spots a roly-poly bug. He looks around to share his discovery with his friends, who are all around the drums. Ollie picks up the bug with his hands and takes it to the drum space. He sets the bug on the carpet and points to the bug. His peers notice the bug but remain interested in the drums. Ollie is not satisfied. He follows the bug for a while.

A teacher nearby wonders if there is a way to build these two interests, the drums and bug, together so Ollie can have a more active experience in music. She asks Ollie, "Should we put the bug on the drum?" Ollie obliges and places his roly-poly on the drum. His peer next to him hits the drum, and the bug bounces up in the air. Ollie is motivated by this effect and starts to slap the drum too. Ollie's interest in the drumming becomes intertwined with that of his peers. His peer turns over the drum to see what it would sound like to hit the drum from the inside. The roly-poly rolls off of the drum, and Ollie doesn't notice for the time being. He is focusing his attention on the drum.

Ollie notices a roly-poly bug and follows it with his finger.

At this point, Ollie becomes very focused on the different parts of the drum and investigates how he can create a contrast in sounds. Without prompting from his teacher, Ollie moves the drum to other parts of the yard and uses a variety of movements to create the sounds. He takes the drum to the trampoline, where the drum surface is at a higher level. He flips the drum over and starts to hum inside of the drum. Ollie extends this experience to create his own sounds inside the drum while holding the drum outward. The teacher nearby creates a scratching sound on the drum surface. Ollie listens. He begins to notice yet another sound and revisits the drum with a different approach.

Ollie starts using his hands again, rather than his voice. Ollie drums the drum with his hands in a variety of places before he notices a drumstick nearby. Leaving the drum on top of a plant pot, he moves away to get the drumstick. Returning to the drum, Ollie starts to explore the sound with his newly found tool. Ollie hits the drum on the rim a few times. He watches the drum with all of his attention. He listens and tries a variety of speeds for moving his arms. Then, he leans in and reaches for the middle part of the drum with his mallet. This makes a different sound, and Ollie stops. He looks and then does it again. Noticing that Ollie is exploring hitting the drum in different locations to create sound, a nearby teacher shares with Ollie that she heard a different sound when he touched this part than when he was hitting the other places.

Ollie hums inside the drum with his friend. They begin hitting the inside of the drum.

Ollie transports the drum to the trampoline and hits the top of the drum from a new direction.

Ollie looks inside the drum.

Ollie holds up the drum and sings. His voice is amplified.

Ollie's teacher scratches on the drum. He can see her silhouette through the drum top.

Music highlights many mathematical concepts for young children to experience and articulate by engaging in STEAM learning experiences. Ollie is integrating science and art concepts to further his mathematical understanding of volume, speed, patterns, and the characteristics of sound. He discovers how to make the sound louder or quieter by whispering, shouting, and using more physical force with his movements. He explores how to adjust the production of sound to different intensities, volume, and styles. He demonstrates this when he tries to make the sound louder by humming into the drum's hollow tube and when he uses the mallet to hit the different parts of the drum.

Ollie is able to learn more about the nuances of sound production as he explores all of these sound producers at one time. He might not be able to fully articulate all of his thinking or make a conclusion related to STEAM concepts, but he is learning more about how to make sounds and the ways that he can manipulate sounds once they are produced. With time, Ollie will use more preferred methods when he wants to engineer "loud" or specific kinds of sounds. These will come more naturally to him because he has had these previous experiences with sound production.

Ollie puts down the drum and drums on the top of it.

Ollie tries a new spot to drum. He is off to find a drum mallet.

Future Possibilities and Reflections

As we consider Ollie's and Zoe's vignettes, we are drawn to think deeply about how we can connect children's movements in play to STEAM concepts. Sometimes we are so busy with all the different tasks around us that we do not fully encourage infants' and toddlers' large and expansive movements in play. We may see the children's movements as just something they do, but often more underlies the movements than we can identify at first glance. Zoe learns a lot when she tries to get off the bike, learning that might not have occurred if her teachers had simply put her on and off the bike themselves. She would not have solved the problem for herself, and her teachers would not have witnessed her learning.

At times, we may want the children to be calmer or to tailor their movements with more control. Although we should consider children's safety, the fact remains that children are learning a lot in any given movement. They are discovering more about STEAM concepts when they follow their own learning trajectories and have opportunities to freely explore. For example, Ollie might not have been as engaged

Ollie drums the drum with a mallet and hears a sound that is different from the one produced by his hands.

in making different sounds with the drum if the teacher had made him drum on the drums. Instead, she encouraged him to extend his science investigation of the bug in relation to the drum. Ollie was then able to design his own pathway to learning more about sound. He not only explored his ideas about the drum sounds, he found ways to make the drumming experience better fit his current learning space. The freedom to move and notice the consequences can be a valuable part of children's development. They learn what can happen with large movements and what spaces in their environments serve their exploration of larger movements.

Movements can make visible a medium's impact on young children's learning. Connecting children's self-expressed movements in music and drama can be profound. Music and movements bid children to integrate their learning into a synthesized expressed experience. The children are calculating what will come next and wondering if they can put all their ideas together in an expression or piece. It is amazing how music is interconnected with the experience and the development of a skill. Exposing children to different types of music and sounds can broaden their knowledge of cause and effect. They learn, for example, what types of sounds happen with metals in comparison to wood instruments. The basic understanding of sound resonates with them as they continue their journeys forward into more complex activities. For example, later on in preschool, hearing the sound of a metal nail go into wood during a hammering activity can provide information about how far the nail has moved and if their hammer was hitting the nail or the wood. Witnessing children's first experiences with sound, music, and expression is a gift to us as it can help build a common understanding of the children's learning.

We are inspired when we see the level of learning that happens when children tinker with ideas. Zoe tinkers with how to move her body in space. Ollie tinkers with different materials to produce sounds and create waves that move his bug up in the air. Their ability to pursue the unknown through hands-on exploration is intriguing. Moving in their environments and naturally seeing the consequences of these movements is a platform for future problem solving. The capacity to explore a medium in different ways by tinkering can be powerful for young children as they revisit concepts. In both of these children's vignettes, we see them connecting to abstract concepts of sound waves and developing their awareness of their place in a space by pursuing their natural desire to move and play.

We end this chapter with a few questions to inspire thinking more deeply about possible extensions to the children's learning.

- What possibilities are there if Zoe revisits her bike experiences at another time? Will she try the same movements, or will she adapt her next attempt from her past experience?

- How might a similar bike experience be replicated for Zoe as she moves around the classroom? Would she be interested in sitting on long, narrow, hollow blocks stacked on top of each other, where she would use similar motions to get onto the structure?

- How can Ollie revisit the vibrations of the drum in a different way than he did with the roly-poly bug? He might be intrigued by feeling the vibrations on his feet or hands when the drum is being struck.

- Ollie was interested in bugs first before exploring the drums. What types of music and sounds do bugs make that Ollie could explore?

- Providing opportunities to explore woodwind or brass instruments might further support Ollie's interests in exploring the mechanics of instruments.

Chapter 6

STEAM Connections with Light

HANDS-ON EXPERIENCES with light distinguish for infants and toddlers how light can be actively manipulated versus being passively witnessed. Naturally, children are exposed to light from the moment they are born into this world. They begin to notice the differences between human-made and natural forms of light as they explore light switches and experience sun rays on their faces on a sunny day. When children utilize light, they discover its properties and connect concepts about light to their own lived experiences. This engagement provides a pivotal learning space for children to meaningfully connect with science and to integrate this newly formed scientific knowledge with their past experiences. Ultimately, children can use the acquired scientific information about light sources to engineer new technologies in their play.

In the vignettes below, we explore how infants and toddlers experienced a light provocation in play. We identify some of the STEAM concepts that emerged in their experiences with the manipulation of light and discuss how teachers can further children's curiosity about light. The first part of the vignette highlights an infant's scientific explorations turning light on and off. Extending from this first vignette, we describe in greater detail the role that circuitry has in young children's learning. Later we discuss teachers' and family members' roles as they observe infants and toddlers using new light materials. The second part of the vignette describes how toddlers investigated possible ways to project light across varied media. Light's properties and its transparency are further illustrated from the children's perspective. We conclude this vignette with a discussion about presenting provocations related to light to a multiaged group of children.

Circuitry: Turning Lights On and Off

We look at how infants and toddlers can explore circuitry, observe electric light phenomena, and design experiences for future learning in the following vignette.

The children, ages eight months through five years, arrive at the light provocation with inquisitiveness and interest. The provocations include lights placed in metal bowls and under fabrics and containers, and shining wide-open in the environment. Each child approaches the light source in their own way, often wanting to touch, mouth, or look at the light source in more detail. While bringing the light sources near their bodies, the children begin to notice that they can manipulate the light sources. This involves turning the lights on and off, pointing the lights in different directions, and covering the lights with the loose fabric nearby.

Anthony shines the light up to his face and observes the light.

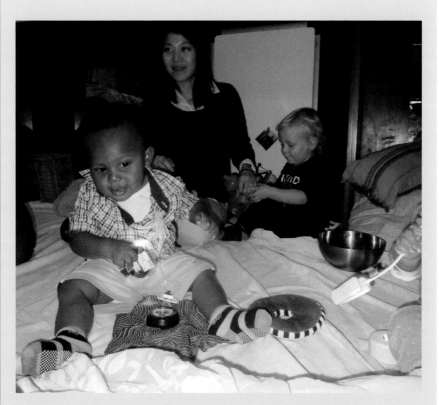

Anthony applies a variety of strategies to turn the light back on.

Anthony quickly notices a light and starts to move his arms around rapidly. He reaches for the light and picks it up immediately. Anthony giggles while looking at the light and brings it near his face. The light shines into his eyes, and he adjusts the light to be farther from his face. From this new location, he can stare with comfort into the light being projected out of the device.

Anthony becomes even more excited and moves his arms upward, causing the light to drop onto the floor. Because this light is push operated, it turns off when it falls. Anthony notices this change and picks up the light again. He brings the light close to his face, and it doesn't turn on. He changes course and waves the light device in the air. Still, no light turns on. He transfers the light back and forth between his hands. Nothing happens. Somewhat frustrated, Anthony seeks new solutions to his challenge. Based on his past experiences, he taps the light on the floor and waits for something to happen. This is similar to how the light turned off when it fell on the floor. He does it again, and the light turns on!

In Anthony's attempt to turn the light back on, he extends his scientific knowledge and accesses the art concept in STEAM learning. Anthony utilizes elements of design simultaneously with his scientific predictions to turn the light on and off. Designing his experiences with the light helps Anthony discover new learning opportunities. In play, Anthony is encouraged to manipulate the light from his own perspective, and he coordinates his ideas to find a possible solution to the questions he is pursuing. Anthony asks what will happen next if he moves the light into a new position, or if he uses a different movement with the light. With each attempt, he is learning more about how to use basic causal relationships in designing new learning experiences.

Anthony is not centered on what didn't work but rather on what designs are possible solutions to the challenge the light poses. As he moves through his design process, Anthony is asking different questions and exploring possible directions to move forward from his newly obtained knowledge. He discovers that his available designs to turn the lights on and off multiple times do not always work effectively. In the end, Anthony uses a similar strategy to turn on the light, involving tapping the light on the ground. The chosen design is the easiest and most reliable in his current situation. Anthony continues to use his chosen design many times to turn the light on and off and shares his creative approach with his peers each time he succeeds.

In this scientific experience, Anthony explores the different properties of light as he directs the light to a specific location and stares into the light source. He is learning more about what light looks like, how it travels, how it can be directed, and where it comes from. He investigates light's properties by using technology that consists of the battery-operated push light. Technology is a tool that gives Anthony access to view more light. He does not yet know how to fully use this technological device, but his pursuit of learning more is giving him some new ideas.

Taking a Closer Look at Circuitry

Circuits involve a simple cause-and-effect relationship that allows infants and toddlers to explore electricity. For infants and toddlers, experimentation with how something works through cause and effect is a developmentally appropriate strategy and constantly carried out by young children. A direct cause-and-effect response to connecting or disconnecting a circuit is immediately evident. The light either turns on or off depending on if the circuit is complete or not. Because young children get immediate feedback when they explore basic circuitry, they are likely to be interested in investigating further.

Infants and toddlers explore circuits and concepts related to circuits each time they turn lights on and off. They engage in the process of turning light on and off through a variety of methods: observing what their peers are doing with the light, and trying different methods themselves to turn the light on and off. Anthony used many movements as he strategized possible solutions to turning the light on and off. Some children may participate by observing other children's experiences before touching the light source.

Zoe tinkers with the light, while Ollie watches how she is using it in order to gather more information.

Teachers and family members can present simple objects like push or touch lights for young children to explore circuits. We can further children's understanding of electricity and light by providing opportunities for children to manipulate lamp dimmer switches, light projectors, and other light sources. Children can explore light's properties in play. They can build new structures on light tables and cast images on the light projector to tinker with the light's brightness, color projection, and encompassment of space. Very young, immobile infants can observe the different shades, colors, and types of lighting. Adults can lay infants next to childproof light sources so they can observe light in greater detail. At some point, the child may reach for the light and notice the shadows cast by this movement. Children may feel the warmth created by the light's electric current when mouthing a child-safe light source. These experiences provide basic foundations for young children's later understanding of specific aspects of circuits.

Infants can observe, touch, and mouth light sources that are childproof. Notice the light from an infant's perspective and how this light setup reflects off its nearby surroundings.

The way that light is explored and set up can promote a strong understanding of circuitry for young children as their learning becomes more complex and they encounter circuits in preschool. There are many parallels between how infants and toddlers explore turning lights on and off and how older preschoolers create simple circuits. Similar methodology is used to encourage preschoolers to connect with the materials more abstractly. The cause-and-effect relationship is still a central theme for learning about circuits. Preschoolers may draw on strategies they used in infancy in their new experiences with light.

Extending Light Understandings across Multiple Media

The vignette below describes how an eleven-month-old uses fabric and metal to alter the light's projection through space. With each exchange, she learns more about the properties of light in connection to other earthly materials. She engineers social experiences and visual puzzles centered around her knowledge of light. Paying careful attention to the material's affordances and available resources, she explores more questions about light. Additionally, we will see elements of art and design in this vignette.

Isabel, an eleven-month-old, picks up a light device and looks at it intently. She notices how far the light is being projected out from the device and turns the light on and off. She doesn't seem as interested in what makes the light work as in how the light travels. She stares at the moving light and intently explores the light's projection in more detail. A nearby light covered by a silk scarf catches her eye. The light's projection is different from the one in her hand. Isabel drops the light in her hand. Next she lifts up the silk scarf to uncover the light underneath. After some time, Isabel places the light back under the fabric. She repeats this process a few more times before finding a different colored fabric to tinker with. She continues uncovering and covering the light with this fabric. Toward the end of this exchange, Isabel picks up a different light source and examines it. The reading light functions differently than the push-button light, and Isabel notices that the stem of the reading light bends. Isabel tries the same methodology with her new light by placing fabric on and off it.

Isabel begins to explore the push-button light.

Isabel iterates her learning by covering and uncovering her light source with the fabric multiple times.

Isabel investigates the reading light and explores the differences between the push-button light and reading light. She manipulates the bending stem of the reading light.

After observing Isabel's interaction with the light source, many questions arise around what Isabel was pursuing in her experience with light. Was she noticing the different colors being projected while covering the light with the different colored silky fabrics? What motivated her to explore this particular part of the light provocation? Did she want to play hide-and-seek with the light, or was she exploring the silk's transparency properties? Or was it both? What should the teachers do next to extend or affirm Isabel's newly acquired experience?

In this vignette, Isabel displays her understandings of STEAM concepts through her interactions with light's projection. She is learning more about light's properties and other relevant scientific information. She gains insight about how a light can be projected through space, and she notes the directionality of light travel and the space that light encompasses. Later Isabel witnesses light being reflected off objects and pursues light's reflective properties with greater detail. She investigates what kinds of material light can travel through. Noticing how light functions allows Isabel to discover more about her world and its natural phenomena.

In STEAM concept development, integration of concepts often occurs while children explore a given topic. Incorporating technology and using textiles and light devices help young children learn more about the properties of light. Isabel uses textiles with light devices to create interesting transparency effects. She is discovering light's transparency property through the textile medium. The transparency feature of light prompts her to creatively design an extension to her learning experience with light. Isabel engineers a peekaboo interaction with the light source by placing fabric on and off the light. She exerts her power over light with each covering attempt and begins to see that she can make active changes to her world. Technology provides a space for Isabel to see her influence on the world and to investigate human-created light.

Facilitating Light Explorations with Infants and Toddlers

We know that very young children may not know all the components of circuits, light, and earth media. But we can be sure that these pivotal first experiences can create a disposition toward how these media will be used in the future and that discoveries will be made as a result. Once children know that they can create changes with a medium, they are more likely to explore the concept with greater creativity, curiosity, and interest.

You can influence the ways children's natural learning unfolds by providing new perspectives on the learning medium. Toward the end of our light provocation, Isabel shows her head teacher her belly by holding up her shirt. The teacher presents a new opportunity to explore light by projecting the light across the toddler's stomach. Isabel intently observes her skin as it turns a different color as the light is projected onto it. An infant nearby reaches for the light to help her teacher project the light onto Isabel's stomach. This altruistic exchange connects the three of them in a shared experience with light. Another friend, Iris, comes to see what is happening. Iris picks up a light and points it up to the ceiling. A giant light circle shows above on the ceiling.

Exploring different aspects of how light is projected through space builds a stronger understanding of what light is and where it can and cannot go. In this example, the children build another perspective about the light as the teacher creates a safe relationship with the medium. They start to use the light as a piece of technology to learn more about their body and skin. The light further illuminates the different flesh colors found underneath the skin. One of these infants reaches toward the toddler's stomach and touches the light. The light source transfers to the child's hand, and a new connection is made among the children.

Isabel's teacher and Zoe shine a light on her belly while she holds her shirt up.

Isabel shines her own reading light on her stomach and observes the light touching her skin.

Iris notices the light being projected off her friend's stomach and comes over to show them how she can point the light source up toward the ceiling.

The children observe the light's effects on their fingers, stomach, and other body parts.

Providing contrasts in how the light projects illustrates light's transparency in greater complexity. The children explore how light reflects through and off materials, walls, metal bowls, and flesh. The light touches the silver bowls and immediately bounces back to the children. This contrasts with what happens when the children shine light onto their flesh and other textiles, where the light projects through the medium more easily.

A four-year-old investigates light and metals together after witnessing the younger children explore light reflection.

Multidimensional experiences are great places for a wide age range of children to collaborate and explore one natural medium together. For example, in this experience, older preschoolers are invited first to watch the younger children explore the light provocation and then later to join them in the learning experience. Collaborative and mixed-aged experiences provide added opportunities for learning to infants, toddlers, and preschoolers. Some of the preschoolers learn through observation of their younger peers and want to replicate these observed experiences when given the chance. Teachers can facilitate a diverse range of skills and interests with simple circuit materials and light technologies.

Tapping into the tremendous power of controlling light can be profound for young children. We see this happen through time as infants learn how to turn the light switches on and off. With experience, children learn more about how light works and how it is connected to their worlds. Teachers and family members can further very young children's curiosities about light while also providing strong learning experiences by engaging children in explorations of simple circuits.

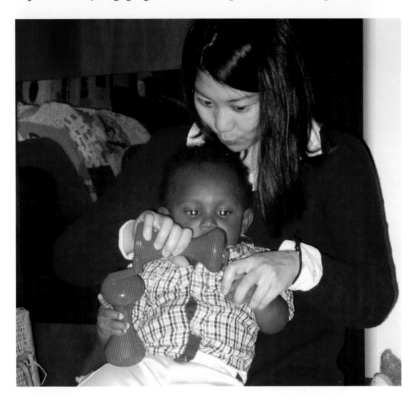

Anthony and his teacher work together to hand-power a flashlight by winding the device.

Future Possibilities and Reflection

Light is a natural platform that connects all learners together in a shared experience. It transcends boundaries and builds relationships with people. In the vignettes, we notice how children and teachers naturally engage in play with each other. They do not know what will happen next in their moment-to-moment exchanges. Instead, they venture on a shared journey to experience a medium and express their joy with each other in each new discovery. There is a sense of trust between the children and the teachers as they explore the medium together. These experiences first start with a teacher's willingness to travel into unknown spaces. This disposition to explore can lead to more stimulating interactions with a medium than simply doing what we have always done with the materials. As Tom Kelley and David Kelley state, "Embracing experimentations can help fuel the fires of innovation" (Kelley and Kelley 2013, 145). These teachers had not used the light materials previously with the children, but they were willing to try it. This stance supports the teachers' lifelong motivation to learn by observing children's learning and connecting it to their own experiences.

Here are few extensions that teachers can consider in future experiences with light.

■ How would children relate to sand and other natural media if these were placed on top of a light table?

■ The children seem to want to share their light experiences with each other. Would they want to share their knowledge about light with their families at a family event?

■ What connections have the children made between shining light onto their skin and their previous medical experiences? Could the teachers introduce more medical play to the children, especially if the children have had recent checkups with their doctors?

■ What does light look like when it is explored in a very dark room or while inside a box? In comparison to the classroom's open space, is the light more visible? Would the children be more reliant on the light source when in a darker space?

■ What experiences would result from the children's exploration of a long string of lights connected to each other?

■ The reflection of light was pursued in the vignettes. How would the children respond if mirrors were added to their experiences with light and to their learning spaces?

■ How could a touch-switch lamp challenge the children's schemas about lights being turned on and off?

■ Children could interact with images cast by light projectors and explore the light's projected size with flashlights and nearby walls. In what ways could the projection of light or light images be explored with infants and toddlers on a large scale?

■ How does the absence of light and shadows inform children's experiences with light?

■ What are the children telling us in their explorations of light?

Chapter 7

Establishing an Environment for STEAM Learning for Infants and Toddlers

In this chapter, we explore how STEAM learning environments are greatly influenced and created by the following four categories: teachers' interests, children's interests, physical space, and culture and family contexts. The approach is embedded in a cultural space where families, teachers, and communities can influence how infants and toddlers interact within environments that promote STEAM concept learning. We share how we can align our own preferences and teaching styles with STEAM concepts and their environments. We reflect on our interests and ways to build a craft for teachers in furthering their own STEAM learning experiences with very young children's learning. Finally, we highlight some barriers to creating STEAM concept environments and discuss the role that culture provides in this process.

Finding the best STEAM learning environment for your space should be centered on an approach that considers all the learning contributors to the infants' and toddlers' experiences with STEAM concepts. This means noticing who is involved and why. Consider a chair. Its four legs support a platform for sitting, moving, and standing. In this analogy, the chair is the infants' and toddlers' STEAM learning environment. One of the legs is the children's interests and motivations to pursue their learning. The second leg is the adult perspectives that the teachers have about a given STEAM concept. The third chair leg is the physical space and daily schedule. Our fourth leg encompasses where we live, the children's community, and the types of experiences we have already had. Communities, families, and culture can give infants and toddlers access to certain STEAM media that are more highly valued than other STEAM media in each particular environment. Using this chair analogy, we can set up the learning spaces from the perspectives of children, adults, and families. We complete this space by providing environmental and cultural frameworks so that learning takes place within a given context. This cohesiveness will establish a sturdy and long-lasting STEAM learning environment that will carry infants and toddlers into their preschool years. If we alter one leg of the chair, then we need to adjust the other legs to prevent the chair from falling. Ultimately, multiple perspectives influence how the environment is set up to promote children's STEAM concept learning.

The Teacher's Role in Environmental Setup

Teachers play an integral role in what is placed in the environment and how the materials are shared with infants and toddlers. They notice how children are using a medium and find ways to introduce new approaches to a concept. Teachers seek out learning exchanges with very young children that are interesting to themselves as well as to the children. With this in mind, it is imperative that teachers take a reflective stance to identifying the impact of the materials and the impact of their attitudes on infants' and toddlers' STEAM learning experiences.

Reflection is central to determining what STEAM environments best fit your setting. Asking questions about the environment's media and the uses of the environment is important; these reflections can serve as catalysts for creating your STEAM learning environments (see table 7.1 for a list of STEAM-friendly media). What media do you feel comfortable pursuing, and which ones are less familiar to you? Are there experiences from your childhood that influence your desire to use a particular medium? What role do you see technology playing in an educational setting? Are you comfortable with young children exploring undefined materials, or do you prefer representational objects, like pretend food, for them to play with?

These questions and more can guide you in building a STEAM concept environment for infants and toddlers. Notice what underlying concepts are interesting to you, and consider representing these in a variety of media in your space. Pay attention to the areas you are less interested in, and consider why that might be. In one classroom, teachers did not feel as comfortable placing clay out as they did playdough. They found the clay to be too messy and sticky in comparison to playdough; they didn't have a lot of experience manipulating clay. Through time, they noticed why some children preferred clay and found different techniques to work with the clay that were less messy. Finding the reasons behind why a medium is uninviting to you can further explain why it is less used in your classroom. Is it because you have less familiarity with it, or do you genuinely not enjoy it?

Sometimes we can learn with the children as we explore a new medium. The guided learning between you and the children can be a journey taken together. Other times, you may find it useful to explore the medium independently before presenting it to the children so that you can anticipate what kinds of learning experiences may arise. Lastly, identify any STEAM concept areas that do not meet your values or beliefs. It is okay to follow your teaching pedagogy and to think more about what STEAM media fit into it and which ones do not. The following table presents possible media about which you can gauge your own comfort and interest levels.

Table 7.1

STEAM Concepts Media	What is your comfort level in using the medium with children and families? Why?
Metal/wire	
Clay	
Paint	
Sand	
Seed-to-table activities	
Light	
Electricity	
Multipurposed objects	
Plastics	
Water	
Paper	
Movement	
Sound	
Wood	
Routines/rituals	
Natural materials	

Exploring media that are less familiar to or comfortable for teachers can be a journey worth pursuing. Using a projector screen or light table may be familiar to some, while other teachers may have limited experiences with them. Gardening and tinkering with circuits may come naturally to some, while others may struggle with these activities. Technological materials and similar media may be nerve-racking for teachers to pursue when they think there is only one right way to use them. Teachers have different skill levels with particular media. Teachers are different ages and grew up in various contexts. They may have memories of experiences with certain media from their childhoods. We see constantly that infants and toddlers are familiar with various digital devices that many teachers did not encounter until their adulthood. Since school is a social space for learning, we should strive to find some common ground for all the learners in the classroom. Community members' perspectives on media like those presented in table 7.1 become integrated in their daily lived experiences. Everyone benefits from being able to explore a medium open-endedly and with a purpose, even if they feel less skilled.

Some of the materials listed in table 7.1 may seem odd or even dangerous choices to use with infants and toddlers. Their ways of exploring new things include putting things in their mouths, dropping or throwing them (to see what will happen), and handling them in ways that might cause injury. What each of us considers to be safe is influenced by our culture. A case in point is a famous photograph included in Barbara Rogoff's text *The Cultural Nature of Human Development* (2003) that shows an eleven-month-old infant wielding a machete to chop a large fruit. In the background of the photo is an adult hovering just behind the baby. This photo shows that there are ways to make potentially everyday tools and artifacts available to very young children provided there is appropriate supervision. In our presentation of possible materials, we hope to demonstrate how everyday materials that children are aware of but prevented from using may be made accessible to them in ways that are safe. Just as the idea of infants and toddlers learning STEAM concepts expands our thinking about what they can learn, using materials that are not specifically designed for infants and toddlers allows us to explore concepts that are not accessible through traditional toys and media.

Developing a Craft

After identifying some of your common interests, consider how you might go about developing your skill in these areas alongside infants and toddlers. Some people describe this as developing a craft. Developing a craft further articulates the value of teachers following their own STEAM passions and play. Sometimes we see this happen when teachers introduce a musical instrument to their teaching repertoire by learning how to play an instrument. Think about the relationship of the environment to your curricular goals; the development of a craft encourages teachers to take on the children's perspective and to notice the nuances of manipulating a specific medium. This craft is centered on the medium or materials just as we might create environments for infants and toddlers. After gaining a foundation with the materials, introduce yourself to some associated tools, and learn how to take care of the tools so you can share this knowledge with the children. As you become more familiar with your craft, you might want to model how you manipulate the medium in front of the children.

Let's take a look at how we could develop a craft for wire. Imagine wanting to learn more about ways to incorporate wire in your infant and toddler classroom settings when you have little experience with it. Where do you begin? Many people have few experiences with wire, but they are invested in learning more about it. Just like the children, teachers learn to bend, cut, and form shapes with wire. Their tinkering with wire may spark inspiration to try a similar learning provocation with the children. They may wonder about the different sizes of wire and create manipulative rattle-like objects. As they manipulate wire, they notice different ways to move the wire and incorporate these new skills into their wire explorations. In the end, the children can watch their teachers use the tools with the wire in front of them, and they now have a new medium to explore alongside their caregivers. The teachers' connection to wire will inform their future practices with the infants and toddlers, especially when the infants and toddlers are exploring their own questions about wire.

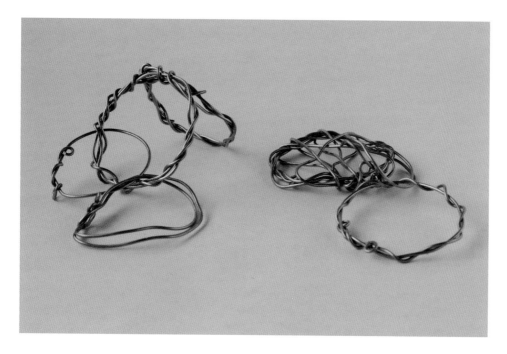

The bent wire created by a teacher provides opportunities for young infants to make sounds with the wire's connected loops, similar to a rattle.

Barriers and Bridges

You may experience many barriers and bridges in fostering STEAM concept environments. Some of these barriers may involve your own attitudes, differences of opinions within your team, or set routines of practice that you have done for many years with infants and toddlers. Other barriers may include being afraid to take risks, finding it hard to articulate what STEAM is to others, and identifying your comfort with using technology with infants and toddlers. Consider the previous example of working with wire. You may prefer to create these materials for the infants when the children are not present so the infants are away from potentially harmful tools in the classroom. This is a valid concern, and you can think more deeply about what bridges you could establish so the children can experience working with wire. The bridge might involve having the tools on display up high where children can't reach them, or presenting the wire separately without any tools. Another bridge might include taping the ends of the wire or bending the ends in a way so children do not cut themselves while exploring the wire. For each barrier, there is usually a bridge for us to take over it that connects the STEAM concepts with children's learning.

Culture, Pedagogy, Community, and the Family's Role in Building Environments

Culture informs how we perceive a learning experience and the value behind a given activity. Therefore, some STEAM concepts may be appreciated more than others, depending on the geographical location, the families' backgrounds, and the school's pedagogies. Aligning our practices with these cultural frameworks has great benefits for infants and toddlers. They will feel more supported and experience the value behind investigating STEAM concepts across all of their environments if this alignment is done correctly.

You can make STEAM concepts visible to families and communities by honoring the children's community context and articulating how STEAM concepts naturally emerge in infants' and toddlers' learning environments. You begin by sparking the families' and communities' interest in engaging in STEAM concepts with their infants and toddlers. STEAM concepts can be fascinating to adults when they notice that infants and toddlers are constantly accessing them in their play. You will learn how to represent STEAM concepts to the community when you gain feedback from the families and community members. After establishing these connections, communities will feel more inclined to extend an invitation to the infants and toddlers; the children begin to learn more about how STEAM concepts are currently being used in their community and family contexts. Each community uses a variety of tools and processes to function, and these basic day-to-day connections can create a strong space for expanding children's thinking about STEAM concepts.

Learning about how STEAM concepts are connected to infants and toddlers does not mean that communities, families, and teachers start something new. Rather, engaging infants and toddlers with what is already happening around them is enriching for everyone because it presents STEAM concepts in a meaningful manner. Family work environments, local community public spaces, neighborhoods, and businesses can be strongly invested in children's learning, similar to families' desire to provide their children with a good education. We will share with you two ways the communities can influence and support children's learning experiences from our own lived experiences.

You should consider building relationships with family members to learn more about their professions and hobbies so you can identify opportunities for infants' and toddlers' STEAM learning. In one of our teaching experiences, the toddlers were investigating light and shadow for a few months. The toddlers tinkered with how to turn on lights, move the lights' reflections to different parts of the room, and change the lights' color with different colored transparencies. Teachers communicated the children's interests with their families through documentation on the walls and their dialogue with the families. Together they learned more about how their toddlers were investigating light and shadows. Families brought in flashlights and other materials to the classroom setting that we used regularly.

Then, one day, through conversations with the teachers, some parents made a connection between their work community and the children's STEAM explorations with light. A group of parents worked together at a health care company, and they suggested that the toddlers take a field trip to their workplace. There the children could tinker with the light controls and stage lighting in the employer's auditorium, which seated over eleven thousand people. In this field trip experience, the toddlers investigated light projecting on a screen the size of two stories. The toddlers moved with joy and momentum across the stage while their shadows followed behind or in front of them. Simultaneously, another group of toddlers were in the control room with light and sound engineers from the company. The engineers allowed and encouraged the toddlers to push all the buttons on the light control panels, and the toddlers saw cause and effect on a large scale when they turned the stage lighting on and off.

Families can also bring their interests or hobbies directly into the classroom for infants and toddlers to discover. They might play music for the children, conduct cooking projects, or build various sources of inspiration for the children.

> One family followed a routine during which the older, toddler brother would always go into his four-month-old sister's classroom to say good-bye each morning. While he visited, he explored the STEAM environment alongside the infants and his family. He often left "gifts" for his sister to play with while he was away in his own classroom at the school. He started out with placing a single block inside each bowl, a concept of one-to-one correspondence that he was currently investigating. The teacher noticed his gift on the floor next to the babies and added to his idea. She placed the bowls with the blocks inside on a lazy Susan, which spun when the infants kicked or swept toward it.

With time, leaving different provocations out for discovery became more of a classroom practice for families. Parents created their own thoughtful provocations and left them for the classroom infants to encounter. The families felt empowered to interact, change, or modify the children's STEAM material presentations with their added perspective. This ultimately influenced what STEAM concepts the children experienced and how they experienced them, and their families were more invested in the infants' explorations of STEAM concepts when they could see their children playing with something they had previously created.

These experiences are real-life, meaningful, and powerful for children. It is difficult to replicate the same light experiences in the classroom that the families' employer provided for the toddlers. However, infants can explore deconstruction with their families' constructed materials along with the classroom materials. Communities can bring the teachers' and children's STEAM learning to a deeper level by adding new perspectives, methods of doing, and reasons for exploring STEAM concepts. Communities, families, and culture open up new possibilities of learning not yet discovered.

Becoming aware of families' perception of STEAM materials and their investment in STEAM concepts is a great place for you to start building environments that reflect the children's cultural backgrounds. Families may not have used STEAM concept materials with their children, and this can create some anxieties for caregivers. They may have many questions about what you are doing and why you want to present a medium to the children. Often families are curious and ask questions because they want to learn more about STEAM concepts rather than being against using them with young children. Give families time to interact with the materials, listen to their ideas, and be responsive to their requests for how they want their children to engage with these media.

Building bridges between family concerns and curriculum design can further extend your STEAM learning environments. Families' concerns easily blossom into new opportunities when teachers creatively find a new angle to approach a STEAM concept that feels comfortable for everyone. In *Creative Confidence: Unleashing the Creative Potential within Us All* (2013), Tom and David Kelley state, "Constraint can spur creativity and incite action, as long as you have the confidence to embrace them" (127). Constraints and concerns can bring new opportunities for the teacher and the families. Without prompts like this, teachers may not think of new activities or approaches to a medium. For example, cleanliness and safety are important in caring for infants and toddlers. Infants are constantly mouthing and trying to bring objects to their mouths. Families may not want their child to mouth fallen leaves or other natural items because they could be dirty or unsafe; however, you can build bridges while still exploring nature and fallen leaves. Begin by considering alternative ways to access this natural medium. The situation bids the teacher to consider presenting media to children with a new perspective or method. For example, you could laminate leaves in large plastic sheets for young infants to lie on or look through. You could tape a leaf up on the window for young children to look at it and later explore the leaf's shadow on the floor below. Additionally, you could place leaves into plastic sheets and put them on a light table for young children to witness the color variations in the leaves.

Regardless of the idea, being flexible as you build bridges that link children's learning to their families' desired cultural practices is a rewarding and innovative process. Having the families join you when introducing infants and toddlers to a new medium that the families may have concerns about can be helpful. Learning more about what skills the families have related to STEAM concepts reveals ways to leverage the families' interests for new possibilities to explore in your setting. It is inspiring when family members introduce a new STEAM material to you and it builds your repertoire of STEAM concepts for your future practice.

Another factor that heavily affects how you establish STEAM learning environments is the pedagogy of the infant and toddler setting. The STEAM learning framework discussed in this book is translatable to a wide range of child care and school pedagogies for young children. Establishing a framework that integrates science, technology, engineering, the arts, and mathematics in children's learning experiences and play is central. Teachers embark on learning about STEAM concepts with the infants and children, tailoring future learning extensions for the children with the school's pedagogies. This framework can take multiple shapes in given settings and can be affected by the teachers setting goals for how they teach children new skills.

The school's mission and beliefs, available resources, and adopted curriculum influence what materials are available for infants and toddlers to explore STEAM concepts. School resources and classroom values may influence how materials are used creatively with children. Pay attention to what your school's available materials are and how they connect to STEAM concepts. When speaking to the children and families, be explicit in your explanation of how you are exploring STEAM concepts with the materials. This will align your school's pedagogy with your interest in STEAM concepts.

You are making connections to what the school and families expect you to do with the materials while highlighting STEAM materials more explicitly. Some of these materials and beliefs can be strongly related to STEAM learning, while others are harder to connect to STEAM. The more you connect classroom experiences to STEAM learning, the more STEAM concepts will permeate the school's beliefs and practices.

We need to consider what open-ended experiences are provided by the materials and give children time to learn STEAM concepts in their play. For example, caregivers and teachers are familiar with magnetic tiles, and children build different objects from these tiles in their environments. Many programs value learning about numeracy, geometry, and the scientific properties of magnetism. However, the curious teacher may want to slow down the process of building with the tiles by not showing infants and toddlers right away how to create different three-dimensional objects. Rather, the teacher could provide the materials to the children for open exploration.

Each child has wonderful ideas that they want to pursue with the materials. By letting the learning emerge from the children, the teachers and families find out more about what the materials have to offer for infants and toddlers. Then, an aha moment occurs in the children's play when they notice a new concept, and it sparks their motivation to learn. For example, an infant could find a new place in the room to magnetize tiles, or the toddlers could witness their peer create a three-dimensional shape for the first time. Then those children become experts for their peers, and the children have a new challenge to try out. The children are empowered to make their own connections to STEAM learning, rather than following an adult model of how STEAM learning occurs with the given materials.

Each community has a desire to nurture the next generation. Consider what types of strengths exist in your community and the skills the people possess. Incorporating their strengths and professions in your STEAM concept environments provides an extension to the children's learning beyond their immediate play settings. This might entail having a construction worker share information about the different lasers, machines, and tools used in their profession, or having the local gardener bring in different kinds of plants for children to be around. In this way, very young children actively experience STEAM learning environments at school, home, and in their communities and gain an understanding over time of STEAM concepts in their greater world.

Considering the Children's Interests and Approach to Learning

Now that we have considered the factors that contribute to the children's spaces, let's take a look at how the children themselves construct their environments. Infants and toddlers seek out learning experiences that are motivating, enticing, and interesting to them. For this reason, children shape the environment as much as their culture and teachers around them do. They show us what they are ready to learn next and the different challenges they want to pursue. Adults should keep a keen eye on what the children are telling them and then use this information to create a challenging, nurturing, and inspiring STEAM learning environment for infants and toddlers.

The climbing structure has loose parts (tires, blue foam blocks, moving ropes, and sand) for young children to design their own climbing experience.

Setting up an environment for infants and toddlers to engage in STEAM concepts requires us to create spaces for all children's approaches to the learning material. Consider how the environment helps infants and toddlers articulate their interests to the adults around them. If the environment is not too prescribed or regimented by the teachers' ideas and contains loose parts and space, the infants and toddlers will share their own interests and their ideas about how to pursue them. Consider where the children are developmentally, and create learning spaces where children can easily revisit mastered concepts and challenge themselves by introducing new concepts to their play. In the photos on pages 97–99, there are loose parts for children to carry around the yard and to build with. A young toddler, who was feeling uncertain about his footing, carries over a square block and stands on it to steadily reach the rope above. This child was able to access learning like his older toddler peers because the environment was set up for his approach to learning. Simultaneously, the toddler's older peers mastered their ability to reach the rope and created a new challenge by swinging on the rope. Infants and toddlers can easily share their next steps related to a concept when they have been given time, multiple experiences with the medium, and attuned caregivers.

Ollie finds a blue foam block and makes a plan with it.

Ollie places the blue foam block underneath the rope.

Ollie easily reaches
the rope and hangs
down from it.

Notice how the children seek out new media and try out different methodologies to rediscover the medium when they revisit their experiences. Social learning experiences drive children's STEAM learning. Frequently, children use a consistent style to access materials, utilizing art concepts centered on design to create common learning spaces with peers. Teachers can account for this approach in their environmental spaces. A reciprocal design exchange occurs when the teacher facilitates the children's STEAM learning experiences and the children design a common language to show the teachers what they are learning. If a child is an active explorer and finds understanding by moving objects in space, consider what this would look like in a STEAM learning environment. In contrast, what would an observing child need in a STEAM learning environment? You may want to have multiple experiences throughout the environment that foster children's discovery of a given concept. This could entail the following: arranging quiet nook areas nearby larger group spaces so observers can feel comfortable watching their active peers learn about STEAM concepts; creating a space where material can be brought to an observing child; and encouraging the child to revisit the materials after the group has finished. It could involve taking the STEAM concept medium outside if the outside space is a calmer area for some children to explore than the classroom.

The water setup involves many different STEAM concepts for active and observant children. The color on the top is different from the colored tubs below, creating a space for color mixing.

Children can use measuring cups and gutters to move the water back and forth. There is space for children to move, observe, and try different activities within the setup.

Infants and toddlers have understandings about STEAM concepts from the moment they are born. These understandings are constantly restructured by their experiences and touch on all the areas of STEAM learning. They acquire a great deal of knowledge from their lived experiences and want to share their understandings with others. Infants and toddlers point to objects they know the names of and show their new favorite activity once they have mastered a given concept. They demonstrate their understandings to other peers in their environments, and they continue sharing what they know with anyone who pays attention to them. For these reasons, children bring their own knowledge and ways of doing things to the environmental spaces. As teachers, we are constantly changing the environment to reflect very young children's voices and ideas. This builds a sense of belonging and encourages children to continue integrating their STEAM knowledge with future understanding of STEAM concepts.

Impacts of Space, Materials, and Classroom Schedules

Let's return to our chair example. The environmental space is one of the legs that supports STEAM concept learning. STEAM concept environments are shaped by the physical objects in the learning space. The amount of space for play, the types of furniture and materials in the room, and the flow of the children's day affect their

STEAM learning experiences. These physical and structural components influence how teachers view a STEAM learning opportunity and the ways that infants and toddlers interact with the medium. For example, exploring water with gutters may not be possible inside but can be a successful activity conducted outdoors. Therefore, we should consider the physical space and how the daily flow promotes or hinders different STEAM learning experiences.

This physical space accommodates water being poured out on the sandy floor and provides space for toddlers to interact with water.

Noticing the opportunities and limitations of the physical space can better equip teachers to support children's STEAM engagements. Physical spaces inform how infant and toddler environments are set up to work with the teacher's curriculum. Teachers plan with their space in mind when they decide when and how to introduce a given STEAM concept activity. Consider what the given space's capacities are and what messages are being projected to the infants and toddlers in this space. This space could involve a learning provocation, a place of inspiration, or a displayed visual setup. Visual displays of media and associated tools that are out of reach send messages to children before they even touch the materials. Teachers may need space to work or places to put children's work in a given activity. Curriculum planning and the use of space continue to inform each other with each exchange.

STEAM activities can be encouraged in different parts of the environment depending on the amount of open area, the types of large objects available in the space, and the natural affordances the environment provides. For example, in some areas the light is intense, while other areas are dimly lit. The space can invite children to create their own building activities and explorations if it is large enough. Indoor and outdoor spaces present different opportunities for children to explore nature and STEAM media. Additionally, in some home-setting and center-based care environments, use of physical space may be determined by whether the children are different ages or same-aged peers.

Routines and the daily schedule directly influence how STEAM concepts are explored in children's environments. Much of infants' and toddlers' learning occurs during routine activities. Teachers must carry out many scheduled caregiving tasks during infants' and toddlers' days at school. Expanding these routines to include intentional STEAM learning experiences with the children creates a rich STEAM environment. By default, a routine links children's STEAM concept learning with sequences, exposure to media, and an established relationship with a caregiver. For example, when infants have their diapers changed, they engage in wet and dry, on and off, up and down—all concepts associated with mathematical and scientific literacy.

Kianna brings her water cup to her pretend cooking experiences. She engages with STEAM concepts (matching pots with each burner, exploring different shaped and sized pots, and designing a cooking space) as she role-plays.

Teachers can incorporate routines in STEAM curriculum for infants and toddlers while considering how schedules can affect when activities are available for children. Some activities, such as manipulating clay, may work better for children at the beginning of the day when their families can be present. Other STEAM experiences may work nicely in small groups or during specific classroom routines.

The materials in the physical space inspire teachers and children to think about and study STEAM concepts. Various STEAM concepts are naturally pursued through manipulative materials. The presentation of the materials can direct or inspire children and teachers to encounter a STEAM concept with a unique perspective. Intentionally placing materials together can guide infants and toddlers to explore STEAM concepts. In time, a new material can be added, and this material can challenge the children's thinking about their discoveries. Sometimes the materials present a different perspective to children and spark a new method of exploring STEAM concepts with infants and toddlers.

These materials inspire children to put objects into small holes, explore different types of media, and roll and balance various objects, as well as to test their hypotheses about how they can integrate media together.

Considering what types of materials are present in your environments and their potential purposes can greatly impact the kind of STEAM environment you are striving to create. Using open-ended materials and natural objects with infants and toddlers creates an intimate relationship with STEAM concepts in your environments. Children can freely experience nature without venturing outside and explore many different ways to use one given object. Open-ended and multipurpose materials can elicit young children's active engagement in thinking about the multiple purposes of the object. Infants and toddlers may be frustrated when they are asked to think about materials with a closed-ended approach. They might not pursue these materials in the future, and they may become withdrawn if teachers prescribe how to use the materials.

Presenting materials that work together across all STEAM concepts has tremendous value to very young children's STEAM concept learnings. They provide opportunities to integrate children's thinking and to revisit different experiences with available media. Children learn a great deal more about STEAM concepts when the materials complement each other than when they are not connected to each other or to the physical space's intentions. Intentional environments suggest to the children multiple ways to find solutions to a given challenge across known media.

Future Possibilities and Reflections

Paying attention to how the space is accessed by children and teachers alike can further illustrate the kinds of STEAM learning that are supported in the environment. The materials and media presented (see table 7.1 for a list of media) determine what interactions between the teacher and children are possible during STEAM experiences. They shape the teachers' frame of reference for what they plan to discover with the children. Teachers facilitate STEAM learning with young children in their shared spaces, similar to interactions in their home settings. This interplay between teachers' and children's STEAM learning is pivotal to finding a balance that fits all STEAM learners, reminding us of the children's and teachers' capabilities to learn STEAM concepts together.

Let's reflect on a few questions. Notice what steps you feel comfortable trying and why. This observation is valuable in constructing an enriching STEAM learning environment for infants and toddlers. An environment that fits the specific contexts and needs of the children and families will inspire you to be a learner with the children in the process.

- What new interests, challenges, and ideas do you feel comfortable moving forward in STEAM learning?

- Do you feel open to trying new STEAM media with infants and toddlers?

- What barriers do you foresee to carrying out your new intentions for STEAM learning, and how do you plan to build bridges over them?

- What is your approach to STEAM learning with infants and toddlers, and what media will you use to pursue this approach?

- How will you communicate with families and involve them in infants' and toddlers' STEAM learning?

Chapter 8

Tools, Media, and Materials

WHEN WE THINK about our greatest learning moments, they are often based on experiences that we have had with media or other people. We can picture where we were, what we were feeling, what we were doing, and who we were with. After reflecting on these learning experiences, we may notice that we had a drive to try something new or curiosity to explore a concept. We may have had an opportunity to revisit the materials or incorporate play to deepen our learning. We may picture a place free from time constraints or prescribed activities. Try to imagine what this kind of experience would look like for the children and adults in your learning spaces. Many enriching environments that promote STEAM concepts have layers of materials and media for humans to interact with. The learning is based on an experience that leads toward a different understanding rather than learning precise details about a given subject.

If we reframe how we see very young children's optimal STEAM learning environments to focus on "the experience," we can further distinguish the need for extensions in children's learning development. We know that infants and toddlers are natural STEAM concept learners, and when given the opportunity, they will make new discoveries with each revisited experience. Keeping in mind their tendency to revisit and rediscover, construct a supportive STEAM conceptual learning environment that embeds extensions in its space. Careful design that includes materials that allow infants and toddlers to pursue already lived learning experiences and to explore new media in a developmentally appropriate manner is essential.

Adults can enhance infants' and toddlers' STEAM concept learning by making essential environmental components visible to the infants and toddlers. First, they can provide a diverse range of materials that naturally lend themselves to infants' and toddlers' learning. And they can facilitate the children's learning in the environment by adding materials, documenting experiences, and creating nurturing relationships with the children as they pursue their learning extensions. After witnessing children interact with a novel medium, we may wonder, "What questions are they pursuing? What are they wondering about when they interact with the materials in this way? What extensions can be made with this experience? What about the medium is so interesting to the children? What can I change in the environment to further the children's learning as they pursue their questions?" The environment is constantly changing to fit the children's learning, while still offering staple environmental media as a constant for children to revisit.

Creating a space for discovery and enhanced learning experiences with STEAM concepts can require adults to consider different approaches to their learning spaces. Teachers may make available tools not previously offered to infants and toddlers. They may alter the flow of the day and how activities are administered in the classroom when a focus is centered on providing "experiences" for children's learning. Young children's experiential learning requires time to explore and the opportunity to revisit their past learning.

Ollie and Chelsea take boats out to the sand puddle. They sink their boats, scoop up water, splash in the puddle, and take turns experiencing the wet sandy medium.

In this chapter, we investigate tools and media that teachers use to create and revise STEAM concept environments. We highlight the types of media that support STEAM learning environments and explain the optimal methods for presenting the media to children in their learning spaces. Lastly, we will explore the possibilities available for children to connect their STEAM experiences across time by describing how to intentionally set the learning space for a progression of learning. Teachers and adults are challenged with finding and implementing an optimal learning space for infants and toddlers. This may be daunting and overwhelming for some and exciting for others. When creating this environment, try to establish areas for experiential learning and discoveries. Creative learning environments are inspired by the people around them and those who are living in the space. Therefore, considering the adults' and school's interests with the children's interests is pivotal to creating greater engagement with STEAM concepts for all people interacting in this space.

Tools to Integrate STEAM Learning in the Environment

In the sections below, we highlight different tools that teachers can use while presenting STEAM concepts to infants and toddlers. We investigate the roles that learning scripts, tinkering opportunities, and craft development play for infants and toddlers. The interaction between presented media, material guidelines, and functioning space are further explored. We conclude the section by reflecting on how teachers can draw on design thinking and reflection to better tailor the children's experiences in their STEAM learning environments.

STEAM learning is enhanced by organized tools that foster young children's access to STEAM concepts in the environment. These tools aid the presentation of materials to infants and toddlers and enhance the environment's design. Infants and toddlers may have difficulties expanding their learning in a given experience when they are in disorganized, inconsistent environments, and when teaching approaches are not aligned to the children's developmental needs. Infants and toddlers cannot use their environments to the fullest potential if the materials are scattered across the room and a specific material is hard to find in play. Teachers can create disarray in very young children's investigations of STEAM concepts by overwhelming children with conflicting questions on how to use the materials. With time and intention, we can identify optimal learning tools for infants and toddlers that increase children's capacities to explore STEAM concepts in their environments. The tools foster children's full engagement in the learning experience and expand their understanding of STEAM concepts.

Learning Scripts

One tool that teachers can use is learning scripts. The term *learning script* refers to the different steps that a person takes when experiencing a learning activity. Children follow a series of steps as they identify and explore new media in their STEAM concept environments. Sometimes the learning scripts are defined by the child's natural approach to learning and emerge in their general disposition to learning through play. At other times, the teacher establishes learning scripts as part of intentional planning of a curriculum that they think will fit well with the infants' and toddlers' current investigations. Children naturally engage in learning scripts because they already follow a series of routines in their daily play and family experiences.

Learning scripts further influence how teachers plan to build connections between the learning materials and the children's cognitive thinking (see table 8.1 for some ideas). Using consistent learning scripts with novel media and materials can promote greater accessibility for learners because the method of exploring the media is already known from their past experiences. Learning scripts can be used when setting up small-group experiences with children, creating provocations for infants and toddlers, and introducing new media to the children. The learning script links the environment with the investigated topics by establishing a series of steps and routines for the learning experience.

Consistently using a specific approach to or learning script for media provides space for very young children to notice differences that revolve around STEAM concepts. Infants and toddlers see how identical tools perform differently with media as they attempt to do the same series of actions from one medium to another. They compare their past learning experiences with their present investigations. Infants and toddlers learn to make comparisons between the media after using similar learning scripts with different types of media.

This circular multipurpose object display inspires children to pick up the objects and explore. The objects are placed so that children can see the aesthetics of size in their observations.

For example, teachers could first present round objects to the children in similar, simple displays as they have done with other media in the past. Because the infants and toddlers are already familiar with this routine, they are more comfortable exploring the media. The circular objects are displayed on a cloth where the children can investigate them freely in play. Infants and toddlers connect their past learning scripts to the circular objects and have some ideas to pursue with the objects. They begin to explore the circular objects by looking for clusters of objects linked together, investigating the objects, and then transferring them to other media in the room. Each child has a unique approach to how they interact with the materials, but the general progression is there. Later the teachers add another step or a different object into this learning script. In this example, a different-shaped multipurpose material could be added to the circular objects. The pointed, angular lines can inspire different learning exchanges related to STEAM concepts. The new objects do not roll as easily as the circular ones, and they stack differently, prompting a new use of the circular objects that can be pursued in tandem with the new multipurpose objects.

The display has the same familiar multipurpose objects presented in the first display. The circular objects are placed on platforms so children can investigate their rolling properties.

Notice the infant's perspective while the child is lying next to the multipurpose objects. The infant explores and observes the objects' shape in a three-dimensional sense.

In this example, teachers carefully think about how children typically use similar round materials before they create a learning script for the multipurpose media. They consider how the infants and toddlers approach new media with other learning experiences from their past. They brainstorm the possibilities for starting a learning script in one particular direction (presenting circles first to the children). They think about what next steps are connected to the multipurpose objects. Adding three-dimensional objects to the two-dimensional objects can change the ways that infants and toddlers see their extended learning experiences because another dimension of the medium is highlighted. The children witness how objects roll, as spheres move differently than flattened circular objects do. In time, teachers start to integrate other shapes with the circular media and add steps to the children's learning script. Learning scripts give space for children to compare new media with past media and different types of materials with the current ones. Scripts offer a space for comparison among materials and media in their environments. Teachers use a learning script as a means to extend the children's learning and connections to their STEAM concept environments.

These objects clustered together inspire children to consider how their commonly held notions of circles relate to the newly presented shapes.

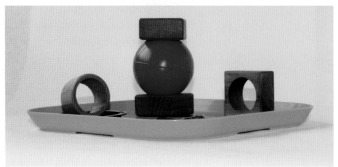

Table 8.1 presents questions that teachers consider when creating learning scripts with teaching teams, highlighting children's approaches to learning, available media, and materials in this plan.

Table 8.1

Learning Script Ideas	The What and the How
Presentation How can we further articulate with infants and toddlers a given medium's properties? What types of presentations and steps leading up to this investigation are needed over time?	■ Combining similar objects together and changing subtle characteristics of the objects over time. ■ Establishing a methodology to present new media to children.
Expansion of tools How can I add media to a commonly held tool that is consistent with the infants' and toddlers' learning approach? What further distinctions should be made between the media in their separate experiences?	■ Using preferred methods of tool use for different media. ■ Identifying different purposes of a commonly held tool through teacher modeling and varied infant and toddler interactions with the tool.
Visualizing the learning What types of media foster the infants' and toddlers' engagements with the learning concept being investigated? How can the children express their understandings in their environments with the media to others?	■ Establishing set routines for how we can further articulate our understandings to others. ■ Modeling the ways we can express our understandings consistently with the children. ■ Actively listening and observing what the children are already telling us.

Tinkering and Tinkering Spaces

Tinkering is another tool that supports children's active and constructive learning experiences with STEAM concepts. Infants and toddlers are natural tinkerers, and they seek out spaces in their environment to tinker. To better understand what a tinkering space looks like for infants and toddlers, let's imagine ourselves in a garage, craft space, or garden. We may find ourselves spending large amounts of time in this environment. What we do in the time that we spend in this environment does not always have a direct outcome. We are learning about how things work and how concepts are connected through our hands-on explorations. Our approach to the experience likely involves being flexible and curious about what happens next. We use tools and materials in these environments, but we do not always have everything that we need. One material in our toolbox may serve many different purposes in our tinkering space, and lots of materials are available for us to manipulate in these environments. This is the mind-set of infants and toddlers when they explore STEAM concept environments. They want to explore their tinkering spaces. They find new and interesting ways to move, observe, and learn about the materials in the environment. They connect the available loose parts, repurposed materials, and media as they tinker in free-play environments.

Providing tinkering opportunities for children can further promote children's inventiveness and curiosity. Tinkering opportunities inspire infants and toddlers to creatively experience different learning concepts with multiple media. By supporting this approach, we are giving opportunities for very young children to learn new concepts that they may not discover unless they explore on their own. Sometimes we may need to set up a tinkering space for infants and toddlers to get them started. In these spaces we may want to incorporate loose parts and materials related to interests that the children are already pursuing.

Let's take a look at how tinkering serves as a tool for children when they investigate wire. The teachers search for media and materials that lend themselves nicely to working with wire. They think about how crawling and rolling infants could tinker with wire inside shelving units. Currently, the infants are pushing materials out of the cubed shelf units so they can crawl inside. Teachers brainstorm stringing objects along wire and attaching the wire pieces to the shelf units. Thinking the sound of wire might be interesting to some infants and toddlers, the teachers create a soundscape with other metals that make noise when touched together. These ideas all reinforce the children's tinkering with wire. Infants and toddlers will happen upon different STEAM concepts while tinkering.

Teachers can pursue many directions when developing a tinkering space for infants and toddlers because a tinkering space is always open for exploration. It invites the children to bring their interests with them in their learning experiences. In the example above, if the children are still interested in putting objects into small spaces, different containers and wire pieces are a possible avenue for teachers to pursue. Teachers continue to modify the children's tinkering environments after carefully observing the children and brainstorming with their colleagues. In time, the children find other purposes for the wire that provide new tinkering opportunities. Teachers model tinkering extensions for the children and support children's own tinkering ideas and innovations.

Craft Development

The last tool we highlight requires us to turn inward and reflect on the types of hobbies and skills we possess. Teachers' hobbies and crafts become valuable tools for incorporating new ideas for STEAM concepts with infants and toddlers. Developing a craft is similar to play and involves investigating how something works. A craft serves as a platform for young children to experience STEAM concepts with a mentor. Developing a craft is not about doing something that you are already proficient at, but rather about exploring something toward which you have a natural inclination and that you want to learn more about and share with others. Teachers usually have some kind of hobby to share with infants and toddlers, even if they think they don't. Developing a craft alongside children can be rewarding for both the teachers and the children. When teachers explore a craft with infants and toddlers, the children learn more about media and crafts, extending their own explorations.

Teachers frequently revise STEAM concept curricula to fit children's specific temperaments, learning styles, or development. Modifying curricula and environments can be difficult if teachers have limited exposure to a concept. But teachers who have developed a craft with a given medium are likely to feel comfortable with different approaches to the concept. They have probably tried different techniques to develop their craft themselves, so they can visualize quickly what activities can be modified for infants and toddlers. For example, some teachers feel more uncomfortable presenting clay to infants and toddlers than teachers who have used clay in the past with young children and have sculpted clay. They wonder what they will say to the families. How will they take care of the clay or use tools with it? Teachers who have developed a craft with clay can easily think of multiple activities for children to explore with the clay and can share relevant information with the children. They discuss the different kinds of clay, model techniques with clay tools, and create new clay experiences. All of this happens spontaneously because the teachers have developed a craft with clay. The teacher understands what is necessary for working with the medium and young children so the activity works and can be modified to fit the children's interests.

Teachers reflect on their own lived experiences and identify ways to implement more innovative curriculum when they have developed a craft. The craft itself becomes a valuable tool for teachers when they consider how the environment should be set up to fit the medium and the needs of the children. Teachers' skills become visible to and valued by families, resulting in greater appreciation for the teachers and their efforts to promote STEAM concepts. Developing a craft gives insight into how to study a new concept and also provides opportunities for families to share their own hobbies with the greater community.

Media, Environmental Spaces, and Material Guidelines

The physical structure determines how much space is available for STEAM learning environments and the types of materials found within these learning spaces. We should be mindful of the different opportunities and challenges a physical space provides for creating environments for infants and toddlers. Some areas are needed for specific purposes, like diaper changing, eating, and sleeping. The space impacts how the children move, what media are presented, and how very young children feel when interacting with the STEAM learning environments. In this section, we establish what core media are used in STEAM learning environments and the purposes that materials have for exploring a given medium or concept. We then share material guidelines and how to incorporate tools for technology in infants' and toddlers' learning environments.

Media

Environmental spaces designed for engaging infants and toddlers with STEAM concepts focus on the media presented and their functions in the learning space. We have described some of these media (clay, wire, water, light, and multipurpose parts) in previous vignettes. For STEAM learning environments, we seek out media that transform, change shapes, and move in space. We hope that the materials lend themselves to measuring, design, cause-and-effect relationships, and active observations. The media should inspire more complex thinking with each learned concept, and they should have multiple functions or purposes.

Below is a list of media that have transformative, multipurpose, and natural processes connected to them. When we consider these media, we think about how they can be integrated and the ways teachers can facilitate this larger learning experience in their environments.

Media and Some of Their Functions in STEAM Learning

Table 8.2

Metal/wire	Bends, creates shapes with force, and makes sound
Clay	Breaks apart, transforms, and represents mental images in physical form
Paint	Promotes color exchanges, sensory feedback, and multipurposed marks in space
Sand	Provides a whole-body experience with shape, measurement, and nature
Seed-to-table activities	Provide experiences where children compost, eat, share, and grow food across time
Light	Connects us to color, shadows, circuitry properties, and differences between natural and human-created light
Electricity	Explores cause and effect while manipulating lights, sounds, energy, or movement
Multipurposed objects	Further define natural processes, measurement, tinkering, and design
Plastics	Provide transparencies to how media can be stored or transferred, as well as the ways that plastics can be molded into tubes, balls, gutters, containers, and sheets
Water	Provides opportunities to explore liquid properties, different states of water, and its fluid motions
Paper	A variety of sizes and compositions further very young children's understandings about how they can bend, shape, break, and utilize a medium with varied mark-making materials in a 2-D and 3-D space
Movement	Extends the child's connection to space, expressed ideas, and large-scale explorations
Sound	Produces different rhythms, music productions, and nature's sounds
Wood	Inspires stacking, building, rolling, and floating, as well as observing trees in their initial state
Routines/rituals	Promote consistent steps for learning and the value of learning a given concept in an embedded culture setting, and provide space for children to create new learning
Natural materials	Used for different kinds of representations, mathematical reasoning, and scientific reasoning that children come across within their environments

With table 8.2 in mind, let's take a look at a group of media that foster infants' and toddlers' explorations of STEAM concepts. Consider a few types of media that speak to you and bring you feelings of joy. You might want to consider what you used to play with when you were younger and still find yourself enjoying. These media are a great start for you to focus on with young infants and toddlers because you will be more motivated to investigate with the children something that is inspiring for you too.

Now think about types of media that are missing. What would be best to add to your learning environment? Sometimes we find ourselves sharing a lot of information about one medium that we know well. We might provide media that are soft or quiet for infants and toddlers but be missing out on the opportunity to explore other valuable media, like metals, large multipurpose objects, or a messy paint. Thinking about gaps in our media environments can help us become more aware of what media the children are regularly exposed to and those that they have yet to experience. Consider adding another medium to the children's environments that fills a gap.

Anthony mixes ingredients together and notices how the textures and ingredients transform with each mixing attempt.

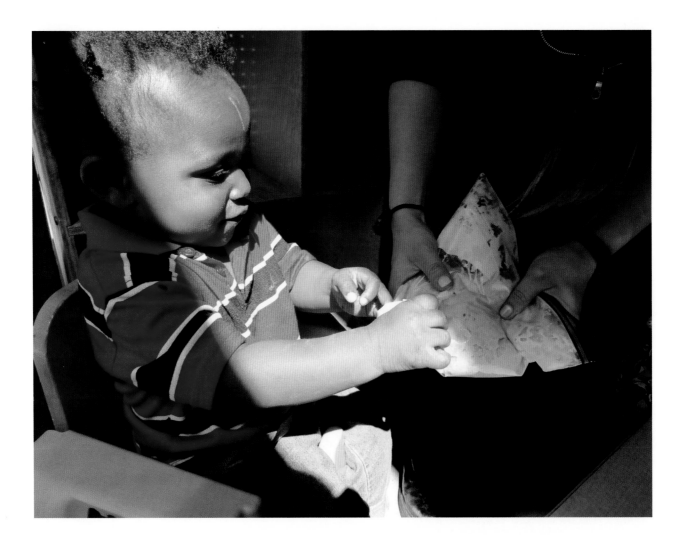

Kianna and Lucy continue mixing the ingredients together until they are fully mixed.

Kianna, Lucy, and Anthony explore seed-to-table curriculum by measuring ingredients and making a recipe for bread to be shared with their classroom community.

Intentionally adding adhesives to infants' and toddlers' STEAM concept learning environments can enhance the children's ability to create extensions with media. Adhesives connect different types of media and include Velcro, thread, clay slip, glue, tape, tree sap, and more. Many times adhesives serve as a tool or source of technology for children to deeply explore a revisited medium. Infants and toddlers learn to incorporate the adhesives in their play with repeated exposure and adult modeling. Adhesives can prompt new learning discoveries across media. Some children find out what types of adhesives work well with a specific medium. For example, children find they can use tape on paper or plastics but that it works ineffectively on sand and clay. The adhesives further enhance very young children's engagement in engineering new technologies in their play centered around a given medium.

In STEAM environments, a strong emphasis is placed on using open-ended materials. Children are encouraged to identify possibilities for using similar materials across the different types of available media. Seeing more than one purpose for the medium's materials can build symbolic thinking and a disposition toward tinkering with the materials. This propels teachers to consider the following: What types of media and kinds of materials do we have in our environments and why? Do the materials lend themselves to investigating a medium? When we look around in our space, do we see a lot of open-ended and loose materials? Or do we see more defined materials, like pretend food or one-way puzzles? Do the furniture and fixed objects facilitate the children's STEAM concept learning? Having materials and media for which the children can discover multiple possibilities, some not known to us, allows children to pursue spontaneous ideas and curiosities. Infants and toddlers can construct their own activities with media and materials if they are less defined. They can revisit their learning across time if the materials and media remain in their learning environments.

Environmental Spaces

STEAM concept learning environments encompass many different parts of the physical space. The adult furniture in the room, teacher's tools, and the aesthetics and presentation of materials play an important role in the messages we are sending very young children and in the opportunities we are providing for them to experience. Consider the types of textures, visual images, and connections from outside to inside that your environments exhibit. Does the space inspire families to engage in the STEAM concepts with their young children?

The adult furniture in this infant and toddler environment is multipurpose and has characteristics that invite young children to explore, such as a secret hideout underneath the end table, visibility through the top, and geometric shapes.

Balls and a zippered pouch can motivate infants to raise themselves up on top of the pillow in order to reach them.

Establishing different learning dimensions of a given piece of furniture provides varied opportunities for all learners in the classroom. Classroom furniture and larger physical objects serve a strong purpose in infants' and toddlers' experiences with STEAM concepts. Infants who lie on their backs next to furniture notice the different textures, shapes, and media even before they can roll over to touch the furniture. The older, crawling infants and walking toddlers navigate within and around the available spaces between furniture. Often a piece motivates the infants to pull themselves up to see what is on top of it.

The steel end table can serve a variety of purposes for children and adults in STEAM learning environments.

You can be flexible with how children use classroom furniture and attend to the different kinds of discoveries that the children are pursuing with each piece. This could involve letting the children safely push over a furniture piece onto its side to investigate STEAM concepts in action. The table shown on page 122 offers endless opportunities for children to explore sound, space, and parts-to-whole concepts. The piece is made out of a light metal that creates sounds when hit, and the lid on the top is easily taken off by children. Letting the children push the piece onto its side gives new opportunities for infants and toddlers to crawl in and out of it. Sounds travel differently when created inside the piece than when the infants and toddlers hit the outside. Toddlers may take the lid on and off multiple times in a given day. This allows them to investigate how a large lid fits onto a base that is the same size as their body. Being open to how children use the adult furniture and paying attention to what types of furniture are presented in the learning space have tremendous influence on what kinds of STEAM learning opportunities the children experience. Please note that the adult furniture may need to be modified to fit the children's spaces or to meet licensing requirements; however, using these unique pieces is pivotal for young children's engagements with STEAM learning.

Material Guidelines

Throughout this book, we have studied the value of integrating STEAM concepts together, and now we will take a look at material guidelines. How a material is structured can foster or hinder infants' and toddlers' creative and innovative integration of knowledge. The constraints of a given medium or material greatly impact the types of interactions the children have with these materials and media. Teachers' modeling for very young children encourages their specific interactions with the tools, materials, and media. Established guidelines for use of the classroom space and materials communicate to children about how they learn STEAM concepts.

Infants and toddlers frequently use materials they find to explore a STEAM concept and investigate questions. While outside, you may notice the children finding all kinds of natural materials, which they collect, bury, wedge into things, and drop. In these STEAM-enriching experiences, they discover new materials that they easily switch their attentions toward and investigate more deeply. For example, the infants and toddlers may notice the frozen water puddle near the water drain on the ground outside while hunting for leaves and then be mesmerized by exploring what they can fit inside or outside of the gridded top to the water drain. Additionally, infants and toddlers may revisit discoveries before moving on to new learning experiences. Some infants and toddlers will want to complete their collection of natural objects before changing course. Teachers that notice and support children's linked learning experiences in partnership with STEAM concepts promote a place for infants and toddlers to transfer their ideas and materials across many forms of media and environments.

A balance is struck between your intentions for the environment and the children's capabilities for using the materials and media in the space. When you set up environments where children can explore across space and materials with limited restraints, you foster very young children's creative and integrated thinking. If you impose too many restrictions on how materials and media can be explored, children may receive the message that they cannot use the materials for other purposes. They can become uninterested in the activity altogether.

There is a place for clear expectations for use of materials, especially if you want children to understand that use of a given medium can be risky if done incorrectly. This situation is an exception to children's typical unstructured play in their environments, where the materials should be safe to explore without direct adult supervision. While you want to give children opportunities to play with real tools, you also have to consider how the materials should be presented. You should first demonstrate how to use the tools while the children observe. Then children can try to use the tools on their own or with an adult very close by. Use of technology (tools) presents new possibilities for infants and toddlers to explore and expand their thinking. We see this happen with toddlers when they use real hammers. They encounter dilemmas and challenges in using the tool (for example, keeping the nail straight when hammering) as they gain real-time feedback from their experience. Note that a plastic toy tool chest allows hammering, but it does not allow the children to build anything. What would we think of putting such toys in a STEAM environment when their purpose is less evident to infants and toddlers?

Consider how you would set up activities around a given medium and what structural frameworks are in place for the activity. Do you let the children explore their own ideas even if they are different from your own? What kinds of guidelines are present for children when they are at play? Are children able to move material from one part of the room to the other? Do you have guidelines for children to follow for moving materials from inside to outside learning spaces, and why? What feedback systems do you plan to use with children who are using real tools that could potentially hurt them if mishandled? Some of these answers will not be clear until you have had experiences where you have to make immediate decisions.

Guiding material and media experiences to promote an active construction or deconstruction of knowledge is a great place to start. Children who see their media, materials, and tools as a resource for building their STEAM knowledge are more likely to engage in STEAM concept environments. Environments that have a place for construction and deconstruction provide endless opportunities for children to explore STEAM concepts repeatedly. These spaces could involve block areas, tinkering spaces, drawing environments, and more. The materials and tools of technology are added to the space over time or even exchanged with other materials. All media provide a place for construction and deconstruction of knowledge in STEAM concepts.

Emphasizing how different types of objects fit together because of their textures, functions, space, and colors can provide more learning opportunities than a pre-assembled toy in the children's space. Provide opportunities for the children to build their own structures in play. Consider what influence their construction/deconstruction play is having on their learning before directing the play toward a specific purpose for the children. Are they discovering other STEAM concepts in connection with their building not yet visible to the teacher's eye?

Try to establish environments that invoke a sense of construction or deconstruction in them. Sometimes children learn more about how to put things back together when they have had a chance to take them apart. Let's go back to the metal end table discussed earlier. Remember how the end table could be taken apart or put together. The piece can become a tinkering space for older infants and toddlers to construct sound in. Infants and toddlers can produce sound when different media are tapped against it. A wooden rain stick, metal keys, and a soft ball of yarn lie on the top of the metal base. Each object creates a unique sound and moves differently in interaction with the end table. As an added benefit, the removal of the top helps children to discover sounds from within and outside of the base. They may want to lay it down on its side and crawl inside the piece to hear their voices echo. Space that lends itself to the construction or deconstruction of children's ideas ranges in complexities, materials, media, and interests.

This end table can be a platform for sound production and tinkering experiences.

Incorporating technology into infant and toddler learning spaces can be simple or complex, depending on the types of tools available to the children. It can be as simple as putting a craft stick in a book to serve as a bookmark or as complex as using scissors with paper. As discussed earlier, the types of technologies should reflect what fits your style, communities' cultures, and media presented. It is a good practice to identify what types of simple pieces of technology you plan to explore with young children and why. Sharing with the children why you see the object as a tool and articulating its functions can further emphasize the role that technology plays in infants' and toddlers' lives. In time, children will develop their own technologies that they create in play. You can validate the children's experience by incorporating children-created technologies in their environments too.

Tool-use guidelines are established to increase the children's capabilities and engagements with STEAM learning as well as to provide a safe, nurturing learning experience. Teachers, family members, and children may express concerns about how infants and toddlers use complex tools in play. The way that teachers present tools and facilitate their use by children highlights how teachers see young children. Teachers provide tools that they feel children can handle in their environments. Seeing children as capable individuals and citizens of their society can prompt specific tool use with very young children. You should reflect on how you want to structure the tool use in your STEAM learning environments. Some tools require more adult direct supervision or added safety measures, like safety glasses. Try not to limit use of a tool altogether because you are unsure of how it will work with children. You can always loosen your guidelines as you and the children become more familiar with the tool.

Digital technology tools provide both great benefits and hindrances to children's STEAM learning environments, depending on how they are used with the children. Hindrances include having too much screen time where children are passively watching the digital tool and not actively engaging with it as a resource for exploration. Some teachers may want to show images on a computer to children who are interested in knowing what a given object looks like. Teachers use technology themselves to take pictures, record, and document children's learning. Children witness their teachers using digital tools for these purposes. Other teachers and children may want to use video chats and email to communicate with parents while they are away from the classroom, similar to writing a letter to them. And some teachers may take a strong stance on not having any digital technology for infants and toddlers in the classroom.

Regardless of where you stand on the issue of digital technology, consider the tool from a child's perspective and think about what outcomes will result from using the tool. Allowing use of a tool may not be a good idea if you think the child will focus on the tool itself more than using the tool for its purpose. Teachers should decide which digital media tools they will model for the children and which tools they will let the children physically manipulate. How to manage the use of digital media by infants and toddlers is a subject of debate, and much research is investigating the effects that digital media have on very young children's learning (Courage and Howe 2010). With this in mind, find technology that infants and toddlers can independently manipulate to solve problems and that will aid future learning experiences. For example, providing toddlers with a digital camera can help you capture what children notice and want to record in their peer-to-peer interactions and learning investigations.

Chapter 9

Reflection and Design
How Does the Environment Function?

A STEAM learning environment can have all the resources needed for children to fully immerse themselves in learning STEAM concepts, but it cannot serve its purpose if the physical space is too difficult to function in. How we use the environment is dependent on the children's and classroom's daily schedules, the given space, the program's logistics, and the teachers' attunement to how the space is functioning. As teachers and caregivers, you need your own workspace to function. You should have places to put objects out of reach from children, as well as opportunities to connect with other teachers or family members to plan curricula. With this in mind, we will explore some of the barriers to having well-functioning space for STEAM concept environments.

We discuss two tools, design and reflection, that can prepare us for overcoming barriers in our practice. We examine some challenges in detail and describe the roles that reflection and design have in finding possible solutions to these challenges. We explain how using design helps us establish enriching and context-specific STEAM learning environments. We conclude this chapter with an example of how you can facilitate and support STEAM learning experiences with paint in your environment.

Functioning

The functioning of STEAM concept learning environments is greatly influenced by basic components: infants' and toddlers' individual schedules, and the flow of a classroom's daily schedule. Infants' and toddlers' schedules and needs drive what happens in their daily routines and play. You may need to be creative in finding ways to expose children to STEAM concepts and play while still managing the routines needed for their peers. In one situation, teachers exposed infants to nature by facilitating an outside activity with a group of awake infants while the sleeping infants slept inside with another teacher in the classroom. Providing small-group experiences of STEAM concepts is just one form of STEAM learning.

Many classroom and individual routines already have STEAM concepts embedded within the activity. Find times in the children's individual routines or brief moments of their day to foster STEAM concepts. Children and teachers should be encouraged to share more about STEAM concepts while performing children's daily routines. During a diaper change, you can talk about wet/dry concepts, directionality, and body parts. You can give children more time to wash their hands and ask them inspiring questions. For example, "Where does the water go after we flush the toilet?" You are going to spend the same amount of time and energy going through the routines either way. Taking time to make concepts more visible to the children and actively observing the children in their given routines can really make a difference.

Establishing your routines and systems to facilitate STEAM concept activities with infants and toddlers readily in the classroom will enhance your ability to revisit STEAM learning experiences throughout the day. It helps to have the materials properly organized and ready to go at a moment's notice. Consider what you need to do this work effectively with young children and integrate these resources into your space. This may involve making the media and materials for STEAM concepts more available to you and the children. Paying careful attention to what types of media are available and to ways to display the media for infants and toddlers in play can help you carry out classroom routines while overseeing children's independent STEAM learning from a distance. Making materials requiring supervision available on nearby shelves allows you to access them quickly when children have expressed interest in them during their play or during an opportune moment with the children.

With regard to clay, for example, it is helpful for teachers to have clay materials on display to take down for the children during small-group activities and then place back on the shelves afterward. Figure out what you need for the end of the activity to run smoothly. Are there containers that you can store clay in that will keep the clay moist for the next time? Is there a space nearby where you can place the children's artwork when they are finished? Do you have resources nearby to document what the children are saying and doing for later reflection?

Overcoming Obstacles

Infant and toddler care has many moving parts. It can be difficult to focus on STEAM concepts while dealing with staff changes, individual children's routines, and classroom management tasks. Creating systems that coordinate the teachers' and children's STEAM learning environments can be beneficial for the whole program.

Infants and toddlers engage in many routines during the day (diaper changing, feedings, and sleeping), and these routines can make up a large portion of your time in the classroom. You may find yourself thinking there just isn't enough time to sit down with the children and explore STEAM concepts. Remember, the children are still learning about STEAM concepts during their routines and in their self-initiated play. Teachers may notice children investigating STEAM concepts across the room while they are changing another child's diaper. Routines that can involve STEAM concepts include mealtimes (composting, trying new foods, transformation of cooked foods), bottle feeding (exploring how much, how warm, and the different tools used to drink milk), and sleeping routines (singing of songs and exploring spatial awareness while resting in a small space). As we shared in the previous routine vignettes, there are bountiful possibilities for exploring STEAM concepts in children's routines.

Providing documentation of the children using the materials in the environment aids in encouraging children to revisit their learning and in showing new staff the children's capabilities. New and rotating staff may not know how a material is currently being used by the children or where media are located if they want to present them to the children. The established learning scripts for STEAM experiences may not be visible to new staff. For example, documentation of clay being worked on a canvas surface reminds the children of how they can use the clay. Images could depict different strategies, such as pinching, smoothing, and scooping, for working with clay. New teachers can reference this image when thinking about their own setups for clay. Documentation helps teachers and children remember what they have done previously with STEAM concepts and inspires them to consider possible extensions to their experiences.

Staff can engage in the underlying STEAM concepts when they know what to expect and where the media are located. Identifying your role in the classroom can enhance how you see yourself in the STEAM learning experience. Visual displays of the media on shelves eliminate having to find where media are stored, and they show families and children what materials are associated with a given medium. Fine-tuning the current systems of your program can give you more time to be present with the children and less time managing what needs to be done in the classroom.

Sometimes children's particular needs influence the kinds of STEAM activities that occur in the classroom. Some infants and toddlers have limited mobility, diverse learning styles, chronic allergies, or sensitive goodbyes with their families that influence how and when you investigate STEAM experiences with the children. If a child is allergic to lots of foods, consider what foods they can have that you are willing to explore with the children. Notice what brings the infants and toddlers joy, and build in these activities to the classroom STEAM activities. You may want to have two types of setups for one activity available to infants and toddlers, better fitting all the children's unique needs. For example, teachers can set up two spaces to explore water and pouring with children by having both a tray of water and a sensory table filled with water. Infants and toddlers who can't sit or stand easily can explore water at the tray while peers explore at the sensory table. Establishing spaces for pouring and exploring water in different settings also furthers the children's understanding of water.

Role of Reflection

As you are considering all the things that need to be done in a limited amount of time, it becomes increasingly important for you to think more about how the space is functioning in your environment. Reflection can highlight what is working and what is not working, furthering your ability to modify the STEAM learning environments to enhance their functioning. Reflection is like a muscle—it gets stronger with use. Notice the moments that do not feel right to you and those that have worked well in the past. What are the underlying reasons why the experience ended up the way it did? Reflecting on your past experiences can inform your future practices with families, children, and STEAM concepts. Reflection supports teachers' predictions of what will happen in the future and gives them a chance to change a situation to better fit the needs of their particular learning context for the next time.

Reflection is a tool that fosters development of innovative STEAM concept curricula and strengthens teachers' growing competence as they implement STEAM concepts in their practice. We can envision the teacher's role as centered around a cycle of inquiry. The cycle involves repetition of trying out an idea and then reflecting on how the idea connects to children's learning. In the classroom, you can reflect on the ways the children use the materials, what parts of the spaces are used the most, and where you think the children's interests will lead next in their STEAM learning. What are the different perspectives involved with each STEAM concept exchange? How will these perspectives align with your own ideas about the given activity or STEAM concept?

Reflecting on our past experiences can inform our future practices with families, children, and STEAM learning experiences. Making connections with all participants in the STEAM concept learning experience enriches the learning experiences and provides a sustainable effort to support future STEAM investigations. STEAM learning environments function in tandem with families' and teachers' input. Reframe the experience with the children's, families', and teachers' perspectives in mind when assessing how your STEAM learning environments are functioning.

Reflection Tool

- What do you already know?

- What do you want to know more about and why? How will you go about this?

- What have you learned?

Role of Design

Reflection and design work hand in hand since reflection can better inform what kinds of designs are the best ones to use in a given learning context. Design draws the teachers' thinking from a place of reflection to a place of action. Designers focus their efforts on how they can better design a given object or interaction in connection to a specific purpose or context. Our task is to design our spaces to better fit children's approaches to and engagements with STEAM concepts in their learning environment. Designing solutions to current dilemmas that teachers face gives children more opportunities to authentically engage in STEAM concepts.

Tim Brown, CEO of the design firm IDEO, and his peers articulate the role of design in educational fields. He describes three steps in the design thinking process: inspiration, ideation, and implementation (Brown 2009). First, teachers empathize with all the people who are experiencing the situation. Teachers are then encouraged to find a solution that fits the needs of those involved in the given dilemma by defining the problem, identifying solutions, and creating prototypes testing the brainstormed solutions to the given situation. The prototypes are tangible models or objects that help people interact with an idea before fully finalizing a design. Designing a space by first considering the perspectives of the children, families, and teachers helps us find the underlying root of the given problem. The problem may look different to teachers than it did originally.

Establishing successful STEAM learning environments requires us to think authentically about what is preventing STEAM learning interactions from happening and why. Stating that a learning environment is not working is not enough. We need to identify why the environment is not functioning properly so we can find solutions to the situation. Understanding the problems with an environment may require adults to get down to the children's level. Take a moment and lie down on the floor like an infant would. What do you see from this new angle? From this perspective, do you see distracting objects or underutilized areas? What types of spaces are needed for parents to engage in the STEAM learning experiences with their children?

Designs are created to solve problems and tackle issues that reoccur in your environments. In the design process, many prototypes of tangible ideas are created and tested by the people who will most likely use the product. Utilizing design as a tool to overcome some of the hurdles to successful classroom functioning can be rewarding for you and benefit your classroom. In the example pictured here, teachers test out a wire prototype to adjust their new wire display to the children's needs and interests. They notice how the children use the small wire pieces before installing larger and more expensive wire mobile setups in the infant space.

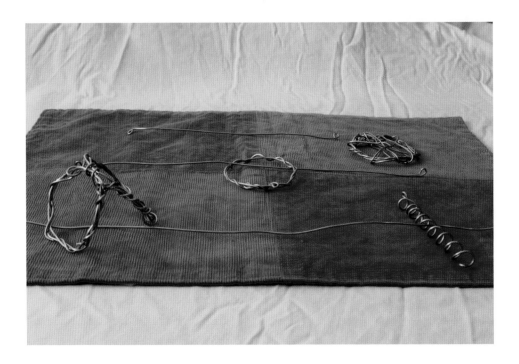

Establishing a wire prototype like this can give you more information about what the children find interesting about the STEAM medium.

Incorporating the design tool in STEAM concept environments can be a preventative measure. A well-designed space prevents roadblocks from occurring in future learning experiences. Good design allows the space to function smoothly. Consider using this approach if you plan to create a big installation for a STEAM concept. As we think about infant and toddler environments, we can use prototypes or mock objects to test how best to set up new materials in the classroom. The prototypical objects depict teachers' bigger ideas and are provided to infants and toddlers for exploration. You can get feedback about the prototype design from observing the children's play with it. In a wire provocation, teachers noticed that the children wanted to stretch out the coiled wire to make it flat. The older infants and toddlers were exploring how much wire they had by putting the wire into smaller containers and filling these containers up with wire. The young infants were curious and looked at the different bends of wire in greater detail. After watching the children explore the prototype, teachers used this valuable information to design the real space in the environment that best fit the children's interests. The process prevents spending unreasonable money and time; an idea is first tested before buying materials or changing the space. Below are some possibilities that teachers thought about after watching the infants explore a wire prototype.

Introducing metal tools with different designs and functions for children can further inspire them to consider how they can use the metal for their own purposes in play.

Children who can pull themselves up to the shelves can measure wire and metal materials and transform the wire's coiled shapes.

Having tools and
resources within
adults' reach allows
them to easily step in
when children need
help exploring the
wire.

The full wire display
is designed for all
learners and has the
potential to facilitate
STEAM learning.

Using design enhances team environments and makes good use of investments to blend STEAM concepts with infant and toddler care. The more people involved in the design process, the better the design will function in the given space. Invite families to brainstorm ideas with you, and identify multiple solutions to your dilemma rather than pursuing only a few ideas. In the end, you can choose a few solutions that best fit your context, but you will have many more ideas that you can use later or in a different context. The design process stresses quickly finding multiple solutions to a given problem first before teachers choose ideas to carry out. The use of design is a valuable tool for modifying environments to better fit a given message and for adjusting the functioning of the space to the children's current STEAM investigation.

Start Small and Think Big: Paint Example

We have covered many important ideas in this book. Now we illustrate how all of this information comes together in the example below. In describing the use of paint media, we show how environments can foster STEAM concept learning across time with infants and toddlers. We describe ways to display the media and introduce painting tools to young children through time. We discuss the role observations, inspirations, and documentation have in the investigations. We conclude our chapter with sharing the importance of family involvement and revisiting past paint experiences.

In this example, the environment is set up so that paint experiences occur over time. Very young infants have limited experiences with paint and are just learning about why paint is important to them. Teachers carefully plan what materials to present to young infants first and how the presentation will occur. Media (paper and water) connected to paint are explored in parallel to infants and toddlers' painting experiences. The children explore the paper separately from the paint before the two media are paired together. Tools are introduced in small, tangible steps. A space is created for children to explore their interests throughout their experience with paint.

The infants and toddlers first encounter their STEAM concept environments when they are introduced to their classroom spaces. The teachers have intentionally created an environment that communicates to the children and families. Messages to infants and toddlers are gently shared in the environment's displays, teachers' dispositions, and thoughtful presentation of materials in the space. Infants and toddlers notice the materials carefully placed around the space in their first moments at school. The children may notice that the paint media have a color scheme similar to their environment's. The walls are painted cool greens, and the furniture accentuates the colors in the room. The infants and toddlers begin to recognize the tools and prepared paints stored in visible spaces but still out of reach from them. They explore the paint media through active observations. They see the images of infants and toddlers using paint meaningfully in wall displays. The environment is set to spark the children's curiosity about the paint media and colors.

In time, the infants and toddlers show their teachers that they are interested in the paint media. They reach for the paintbrushes located on the lower shelves and manipulate the tools in play. They may choose an art board book as their favorite book to read before sleeping. Some of the older infants and toddlers point to the unreachable objects they have become curious about. The teachers take note and sometimes take down the materials for the children to explore under their supervision. Teachers may swirl the paint in the glass jars to show the children how paint moves. At this time, teachers have the opportunity to explain what the children are curious about and share other features of the paint media. The paint display is visible to everyone and illustrates a pathway for those who want to pursue the paint media in a more skillful practice. Canvas, paper, watercolors, and different types of brushes and techniques are displayed. Let's take a look at some images to further identify what this shows the children.

The children can see multiple media from their perspective: paint, watercolors, paper, wood, tools, and ceramic paint containers.

Various types of paintbrushes and rice paper are presented on the bottom shelf; the display encourages children to use the brushes with the paper.

An aesthetics design associated with color and technique is present on the middle shelf, where children can tinker with the color combinations (color swatches, Rubik's cube, artwork).

Canvas and colored paint jars (two primary and one secondary color) are displayed to inspire color mixing and are readily available for teachers to bring down to the children's level.

In this shelving setup, three different layers display paint media. The bottom shelf is reachable so that mobile infants, toddlers, and siblings can discover paintbrushes and paper and use these materials in their play. The middle shelf has a chosen color palette of paints that the teachers plan to focus on first with the children. Different painting techniques and color shades are presented to the children. The top shelf holds what a professional painter might use. Jars of paint are ready to be used at the right time by the children. Paper, canvas, and ceramic containers nearby are available to be used with the paint. Although the children may not experience all of these materials in their environment right away, seeing what comes next is helpful to them if they choose to pursue it. Next to the shelves is a basket of larger, rolled-up papers with different textures and consistencies.

The visual setup extends into infants' and toddlers' learning progression with the STEAM media. Children access different parts of the setup over time, and they begin to construct understandings about the paint medium and its tools. In the beginning, teachers place infants on or near large sheets of paper that have different properties for the infants to identify. These sheets might include crackling paper, thin rice paper, thick cardboard pieces, and rolls of transparent plastic. Some of the infants kick with joy as they notice the sounds their movements make while being placed on the crackly paper. Others prefer to bend or pull the paper closer to them. They notice the paper moving in connection to their own movements and watch its texture change when the sun peeks from behind the clouds. The infants are learning more about the properties of paper and how it can be manipulated separate from the paint. After they have this understanding, they are given a chance to paint on the paper.

At the same time, children have paintbrushes accessible to touch and manipulate in play. They gain experience holding the dry brushes in their hands, and their muscles become more developed. The infants explore how they can use the brushes as tools. They use them to push objects away from them and to reach for higher objects. Later they begin stroking the brush against the paper, similar to painting. These activities indicate to the teacher that the children are ready for the next steps with the paint medium.

The teachers first explore painting with water. They take the children and paintbrushes outside and demonstrate how marks can be made on flat rocks. The children revisit this experience many times and even try painting water on paper. The water dries over time, and the children continue painting the water over and over. We find the activity interesting, and families participate by creating messages for their children by also painting with the water. The experience brings up topics of nature, sun, water properties, and more. Toward the end of these routine revisited experiences, the infants and toddlers are ready for a particular color of paint.

An example of a simple setup containing paper, a paintbrush, and a water container for children to manipulate in their water-painting experience.

In this example, teachers consciously place emphasis on exploring the STEAM media open-endedly, allowing the infants to tinker with the paint medium. Tinkering becomes a part of the children's routines at school, and the paint medium serves as a vehicle for future learning experiences across all STEAM media. The teachers model some of their own painting experiences with the children and routinely point out the different shapes, lines, and techniques displayed in the children's and families' water-painting activities. They do not ask the children to create specific shapes but rather point out the kinds of marks that can be made. In this way, the teachers are promoting more tinkering with the water and brushes so that the children feel comfortable making different kinds of lines in their future mark-making activities.

Using tools with intention refines how children access tools and models different strategies for infants and toddlers. The teachers introduce one tool at a time, and they give the children time to revisit the tool in play. The teachers model appropriate guidelines for the tools and are responsive to how the infants are using them. As the children use the tools, teachers share with the children and their peers that they notice their friends using the tools. The teachers are not on a set schedule to introduce the tools; they follow the children's lead. After the children have an understanding of a tool, the teachers add another medium or tool to the process. We saw this progression when the teachers connected water with paintbrushes. Later they added another medium (paint). Teachers can gradually add different tools and media to a given experience over time, but they should consider starting out simple first. If media and tools are presented together, the emphasis may be placed on the tool rather than on the investigative topic. Therefore, give children a chance to explore the tool before asking them to pair it with a medium.

After children have a stronger understanding of the water-painting concept, the teachers brainstorm how they can use learning scripts to introduce using paints to the children. Earlier, teachers set up an experience painting with water on the flat rocks outside. This allowed the children to investigate making marks on the rocks with water, an activity similar to painting on paper. The teachers continue the children's water-painting journey by placing small containers of water inside the classroom on tables so children can explore water painting on paper. The learning script for how the children explored water painting with rocks is applied to painting on paper. The infants recognize the experience with water and paper as similar to their past experiences and easily engage in the new experiences. They dip their brushes into the ceramic containers and place marks on the paper. Family members join the children in their mark making, creating a dialogue between the children and families as they take turns dipping their brushes into the water. Teachers follow a similar learning script with the paint as they did with the water. Paint is placed inside the same containers and presented with similar paper for the children to explore at the table.

This progression allows for children and teachers to attend to the different properties that paint and water present in STEAM learning experiences. The infants notice how water moves with the paintbrushes and that the paper tears when it becomes too saturated with water. By the time the children experience the paint, they can extrapolate from their experiences and have some ideas about what they think will happen. The infants and toddlers are less inclined to smear the paint over their bodies or become fixated on the tools when a series of steps leads to the experience. Instead, they know how to purposely use the paint with tools and other media. Notice that the children do not need to learn about a whole new set of tools, routines, or scripts for each experience. They are ready to creatively extend their thinking across multiple media and to present their own suggestions during the exchange.

Teachers develop their craft as they engage in the water-marking experiences and create curriculum for the paint medium. They observe the different brushstroke techniques associated with making marks on paper just like the children do. Through trial and error the teachers learn how much water can be applied to the paper before it rips. This prompts them to experiment with different kinds of paper to find what is best suited for the children's activity. Teachers add tools to facilitate their paint activities with infants and toddlers. They tape the paper's borders to the table to prevent the paper from being pushed off. Teachers recognize what kinds of schemas the children are forming with the STEAM media, and they introduce new media to the children's paint activities. They keep some aspects constant (using the same dipping containers, for example) while changing a few others. Different kinds of paint and paper increase the complexity of the experience while the routine steps for the media are maintained.

We learn a lot by observing young children's thinking in action and reflecting on our observations. We can use this knowledge to set up more enriching STEAM learning environments for infants and toddlers. In the paint example, teachers think about the different media and their possibilities first before presenting the paint to the children. Their observations of the children's interests, how infants are using the tools, and what they are not doing inform the teachers' next steps. Teachers think about how their use of the space facilitates STEAM concept learning through the paint medium at each iteration. Making marks on rocks with water is first introduced to the children outside, where children can pour the water on the ground. When the children show more purpose in their use of paintbrushes and water, the teachers introduce paper for water painting inside.

The space and its functioning evolve with each reflection and iteration. After reflecting, the teachers set up the water-marking activity inside. Paper, paintbrushes, and water are placed on a table for the infants to discover. The teachers' reflections further inform their intentions for their next steps; they introduce water-painting activities to small groups at a table during infants' free play. Reflection can guide our future steps and next intentions with very young children, creating visibility about what is currently working.

Over time, teachers incorporate their reflections into design changes in their environments. Teachers are prompted to design a new painting experience after noticing a change in the way the children are viewing their work. Their reflections indicate that the infants are taking ownership of their painting spaces, and they consider setting up separate, individual spaces so children can have more individualized art experiences. The design would include places for the many painted pieces of paper to be stored so they can be displayed in the room and returned to families.

Infants and toddlers develop at a fast pace, and this requires a constant change in the design of their STEAM learning environments. Because all the children have their own learning trajectories, it is important to have different levels of learning opportunities in the STEAM concept environments. Differently skilled infants and toddlers want challenges and places for mastering skills in a given medium. In the paint example, the children may transition from rolling to sitting to crawling to standing and walking as they explore the paint medium. Additionally, infants and toddlers follow their own movement trajectories, and they are not all going to be doing the same thing at the same time. With this in mind, think about how you and family members can design a space and activities to provide equitable access to painting experiences for all the children in their classroom.

Unpacking the role of design highlights the value that design has for infant and toddler environments. Design requires you to consider alternative perspectives and to act on new information in the process. In the paint example, teachers may want to interview families and ask them what their ideas are for the paint medium. They could look at other classroom spaces that have an established painting space and consider which aspects of this environment would be a good fit for their own spaces. Teachers who role-play being an infant, a teacher, and a family member in their paint medium environments identify what will work or not work for their community members. We saw how teachers utilized the whole school space as their classroom for their painting activities. They engaged in outside and inside water-marking experiences, had materials for painting that involved all skill levels presented on shelves, and incorporated the families into their mark-making activities.

Documenting the experience can build deeper understanding of the medium and its environment with families, teachers, and children. It makes the learning visible to the community and to ourselves. When we reflect on an image or concept, we can explore it in greater detail the next time. There may be concepts the children are not seeing but the teacher is observing and wants to make visible to them. This could include different styles of painting that their peers are doing, such as dotting, side strokes, or thick lines. Teachers could take pictures of these marks, label them, and compile them in a book for families to read at school with their children. Looking at the book may inspire children to try painting different shapes or styles of lines in their future painting.

Figure 9.1 illustrates how a **STEAM** medium expands into other media and tool uses over time.

Figure 9.2 depicts how the provided example extends tool use and **STEAM** concept explorations across **STEAM** media from its original paint medium.

In concluding this chapter, we must emphasize that environments are constantly changing, and these changes influence STEAM learning for infants and toddlers. We know that infants and toddlers are natural explorers who are searching for STEAM concepts to investigate. What we do not know is what particular setups, activities, and media will resonate for a particular group of children and teachers. The ways that we set up our environments and refine their spaces impacts how accessible this learning is for infants and toddlers to experience. The paint example illustrates one attempt to facilitate infants' explorations of the paint medium. Figures 9.1 and 9.2 illustrate frameworks for teachers to uncover their own STEAM concept and media investigations in the future.

Reflection and design support how we nurture STEAM learning environments and why it makes sense for the learning community to have STEAM concepts presented to them in a particular way. Reflection helps make visible the different types of approaches in a STEAM learning environment and assists teachers in finding their own pathways with STEAM concepts and media. Design integrates reflection throughout the process, and it explores possibilities for enhancing the space's functioning for the people involved. As teachers and caregivers, we strive to create equitable STEAM learning experiences for all learners. Teachers want to find ways to facilitate children's progression of learning rather than to teach prescribed concepts isolated from children's interests. Design and reflection construct a space for equity and support lifelong STEAM learning. They provide insight into what types of experiences should be pursued to promote infants' and toddlers' STEAM learning experiences.

Chapter 10

What Next?
STEAM in Preschool

Now that we have examined and discussed STEAM concepts for infants and toddlers, we want to take a look at what can lie ahead for children and their learning about STEAM concepts in the preschool years. How can we build on the curiosity and developing expertise of babies and toddlers? How can we support young children's interest in the natural and aesthetic world to encourage the further development of these concepts?

Preschoolers (two- to five-year-olds) have developed physical, social, emotional, and cognitive abilities that they use in making sense of the world around them. Piaget's massive body of work investigating children's scientific and mathematical understandings (Inhelder and Piaget 1958, 1964; Piaget 1952, 1969; Piaget and Inhelder 1967, 1974; Piaget, Inhelder, and Szeminska 1960) looks closely at how young children develop notions about geometry, number, logic, time, space, movement, and probability. This work is fascinating in that it describes a succession of approximations that children make as they come to understand these basic concepts about the world. However, this work is not very useful for early childhood educators because for the most part, it maintains that young children are not able to make *logical* sense of these concepts, that they tend to look only at their *appearances* and do not think about the *relationships* between the different aspects of the problems that are presented to them. Our experiences with young children show that indeed they do construct ideas and theories about the world around them, putting these ideas into relationship with one another. Developmental psychologist Alison Gopnik (2012) has found that young children test hypotheses against data and make causal inferences, creating experimental situations. Most important is their developing ability to represent their ideas and explore their questions in multiple ways. Educator Lella Gandini (2012) refers to the "hundred languages of children" to denote the many different modes they have to make sense of the world. Thus, preschoolers will continue to build their notions of STEAM concepts given the appropriate opportunities and structures. The work that is begun with infants and toddlers can be built on and extended both through naturally occurring events and specific curricular decisions.

Infants and toddlers are very much "in the moment" as they discover their worlds. While they set problems for themselves to solve, these challenges are usually immediate in nature. As children get older, they begin to plan several-step problem solutions. For example, they build complex structures with a variety of building materials—something that involves both design and engineering concepts. They learn to anticipate balance and weight with the materials, and how they will work together. They envision what they want to do and can take several steps to achieve their goals.

Thus, the role of the teacher changes. With infants and toddlers, teachers are right there supporting their attempts and their interests. While toddlers interact with one another and sometimes challenge each other with different problems, for the most part it is the teacher who suggests a different direction or follows up on the baby's or toddler's effort. An example of toddlers helping one another is described in the clay vignette, where Avery and Kieran attempt to stack clay cubes one on another. Here the teacher is supportive of their work together and does not interfere when they want to combine materials from other parts of the classroom. This example forecasts the ways that preschoolers interact with one another. Preschoolers can make elaborate plans and realize them, given teacher support and encouragement as well as leadership. The key is listening to the children in your care and following up on the ideas you see and hear expressed, wondered about, and questioned. We have shown how much we can learn about babies' and toddlers' problem setting and problem solving by watching them and interacting with them. The same is true of preschoolers. However, we can extend our facilitation of children's learning by encouraging them to represent their ideas in multiple ways and by keeping track of how their ideas change.

In Reggio Emilia preschools, a hallmark of the work the teachers do with children is the documentation of children's thinking processes and ideas, through teacher observation, recording, and inquiry and through children's representations in different media of their thinking and understanding. Teachers follow children's interests in setting up provocations that result in children's deep investigation of natural and social phenomena. For example, in a Reggio school, teachers set up hourglasses with colored sand that children could observe. At the same time, they gave them cameras to take pictures of different moments as the sand was moving through the hourglass. This activity was part of an exploration of the notion of time. When the children took pictures of the hourglass moment by moment, they were then able to look at the photos and compare them to further observations of the sand passing through the hourglass. The photos served as a reminder of what had happened *before* and as a spur to help the children reflect on what might happen next with the hourglasses (Reggio Children 2011). Thus, once the children have begun an investigation or project, the teachers continue to pose new questions or problems to the children; they remind them of what they said *before* and ask them what they think now and why. They encourage the children to share their ideas with one another so that negotiation and discussion about projects becomes a regular routine. These discussions push everyone's thinking forward, no matter what the concept being investigated (Reggio Children 2011).

In a visit to Reggio Emilia in 2008, I (Linda) observed both the purposeful planning across age groups of an ongoing phenomenological investigation, and how the teachers encouraged the children to reflect on the problem. There were three classrooms serving children aged two through five. It was toward the end of the school year, and in each classroom a table was set with a vase of flowers along with different materials for making a representation of this vase of flowers. The floral arrangement was particular to each classroom. For the youngest children, the vase was clear glass, and all of the flowers were red poppies. The materials provided for representing the vase of flowers were paper and different colored markers. For the middle-aged children, the vase was again clear glass, but the flowers were different colors and varieties, although they were all wildflowers. The materials in this case included small squares of tissue paper, construction paper, glue, and scissors, as well as markers and paper, encouraging, but not requiring, children to make a collage representation of the model. For the oldest children, the vase was made of opaque pottery, and the flowers were again a bouquet of wildflowers. In this situation, the children were provided with watercolors, brushes, and paper. This curricular setup represented deep reflection on the part of the teachers, who had considered different constraints and demands for children in representing the flowers. For example, using a clear vase so that children could see the whole flower, head and stem, in the two younger classrooms gave way to using an opaque vase where children would have to envision the hidden portion of the flowers. Another aspect was using wildflowers that were gathered in the fields surrounding the school and in the school play yard. The activity was part of an ongoing investigation into the natural context in which the school was situated (which was out in the country with fields of wildflowers available to be visited).

At the end of the morning, I sat in on the reflection meeting that was held in the classroom of the youngest children. All twenty-five of the children were sitting attentively, focused on the teacher and their classmates. Since it was the end of the school year, most of these children were three years old or approaching three. The teacher had a stack of the pictures that children had made. She held them up one by one and invited each child to come up and explain or present her picture. (Not every child had chosen to do this representation, but there were about ten pictures to be viewed, and not every child chose to share something.) The first child who chose to come up had created a picture that had about ten poppies represented with long green stems, a red blob at the top, and a small black circle in some of the red blobs. The flowers were all in a line, and there was no representation of the container. However, it was very clear that these were flowers, and most of the available space on the paper had been used. The teacher asked the child about the drawing, but she shook her head, refusing to say much. The teacher thanked her and invited the next student to come up. His drawing was on a similar large piece of paper, but his figures took up no more than a tiny space in the middle of the paper. He had three small colored dots on top of short brown lines, all drawn close together. Again, there was no representation of the vase. The teacher invited him to explain his drawing. He had a lot to say. He waxed eloquent about what he thought about the flowers and why he had drawn them the way he had. The teacher pulled out her notes from an earlier discussion and asked him about something he had said before making the drawing. (All this conversation was in Italian, but the content was evident.) She asked him if he still believed what he had said before. He launched again into a long explanation of why he now believed something different and how he had represented it in his drawing, pointing to different aspects of the tiny flowers represented on his paper.

This extended description of what happened exemplified what I saw resulting from the teachers' careful planning of the activity and subsequent questioning of the children. These intentional moves on the part of the teachers resulted in children's deeper understanding of the flowers, the placement of the flowers in a container, and the different modes of representing the flowers. When the teacher asked the second child to reflect on what he had thought before, using his own words to remind him of what he had said earlier, his response indicated more reflection on the problem at hand and his recognition of how his own ideas had changed. Provoking this kind of reflection in children, as well as presenting them with interesting problems to solve, supports the continuing development of STEAM concepts, including representation of ideas aesthetically and scientifically. The infant and toddler centers and the preschools in Reggio Emilia have a vast library of documentation that illustrates the different ways children approach problems, investigate them, and reflect on them. Their curricula always involve an integration of some STEAM concepts in the work.

When children are encouraged to reconsider their ideas and to represent them in multiple media for multiple audiences, their ideas change, becoming more complex and more flexible. When they are confronted with what they thought previously, they reflect on those ideas and compare past and present understandings. They have the opportunity and expectation that they will share their ideas and thinking with one another and that their ideas will be valued and respected. The context encourages and expects that children will collaborate on solving problems and figuring things out together.

I had another opportunity to observe an example of such collaboration in Reggio when I visited in 2009. In this instance, I sat with a group of other visiting educators viewing a video of a group of four five-year-old boys creating a table and four chairs out of clay. The video was unedited, although the teachers had provided subtitles so the non-Italian-speaking audience could understand the children's conversations and the teacher-children dialogue. The teacher had suggested to the team of children that they build a clay replica of the table and chairs they were using. While this might not seem like a very exciting challenge, the boys responded with enthusiasm. The first thing they did was *each* build a table and a chair. After completing the task, they realized they had enough chairs but too many tables. The next problem was what to do. They could have used one of the tables they had made, but instead they decided to build a new table and each do one part of it. One child directed the others, and they complied with his instructions. Occasionally the teacher made an observational comment, but for the most part she observed. The boys encountered problems, such as making a table large enough for their four chairs, realizing that the four chairs were different sizes and would not all fit at the table in the same way, finding ways to make the legs of the table support the top of the table, engineering chairs that had backs that would stay vertical and legs that would support the whole structure, and so forth. In each instance, they were grappling with both STEAM concepts and social concepts: engineering a table and chairs that fit together, creating a table and chairs that were aesthetically pleasing, making sure they had the right number of chairs and tables for the problem they were solving, figuring out how to make the clay do what they wanted it to, figuring out how to be inclusive and supportive of one another's efforts. One could list other concepts as well, but these illustrate the breadth of the problem areas they were addressing.

Developmental psychologists Constance Kamii and Rheta DeVries (1993) and DeVries, Betty Zan, Carolyn Hildebrandt, and colleagues (2002) present important suggestions and ideas about curricula for preschoolers that support the further development of STEAM concepts. They emphasize the different kinds of knowledge that children explore in the process: physical, logico-mathematical, and social. In particular, they use physical knowledge activities to help children build their understanding of all three areas of knowledge. They describe two important aspects of children's engagement in physical knowledge activities. One aspect involves the child's *action* in investigating the problem; the second involves the child's *observation* of what occurs. They differentiate the sorts of activities that children engage in: those in which the child's action is primary (as in the movement of objects) and the child's observation is secondary (watching what happens when the objects are moved), and those in which the child's observation is primary (as in changes in objects) and the child's action is secondary (a similar action can result in different results depending on the nature of the objects used). Understanding the differences between these sorts of activities can help teachers think about their curricula in purposeful ways that include an understanding of the STEAM concepts involved and how these concepts are applied. Thus, for example, giving children the opportunity to build ramps and pathways (DeVries and Sales 2011) primarily involves children's actions and secondarily involves their observation (as they observe what happens from their actions). In contrast, cooking activities involve children's observation of what happens when they mix and then heat different kinds of substances; in these activities observation is primary, and mixing is secondary (since it could involve many different substances).

Children's STEAM concept explorations in their preschool years reflect preschoolers' belief that they can create change in their world. How they see themselves in connection to STEAM concepts can enhance or hinder their future STEAM learning experiences. Preschoolers create new social rules to their play, initiate new learning experiences, and want to be a part of the greater community. We can connect children's desire to create change with the greater community by inviting community members into their STEAM learning experiences. For example, interviewing a computer scientist about what a software developer does at work can give children a greater understanding of how computers, electricity, and code work, enabling them to be more than passive consumers of STEAM concepts. Connecting preschoolers' STEAM learning experiences to real-life events can be empowering for preschoolers.

Preschool teachers need to observe and note carefully the problems children set for themselves and the solutions children discover from those problems set by the teachers. Encouraging children to represent their problem ideas and solutions in a variety of media will promote reflection for children and teachers, show children that their ideas are taken seriously, and allow teachers the reflection space for considering what aspects of a problem children are actually noticing. Teachers can then respond appropriately, supporting children's investigation, suggesting new pathways, and challenging children's conceptions. When children do *not* succeed in their goals, teachers can help them understand what they have learned from trying and learn to see not achieving a goal not as a failure but as a knot to be disentangled or a further challenge to be investigated. Preschoolers are capable of extended investigations and reflections. In pursuing STEAM concepts, teachers need to observe and record children's observations and wonderings while also encouraging their reflection through representation of their discoveries and further questions.

References

Ainsworth, Mary D. 1982. "Attachment: Retrospect and Prospect." In *The Place of Attachment in Human Behavior,* edited by Colin M. Parkes and Joan S. Hinde. New York: Basic Books.

Baillargeon, Renée. 1994. "How Do Infants Learn about the Physical World?" *Current Directions in Psychological Science* 3:133–40.

Bowlby, John. 1969. *Attachment.* Vol. 1 of *Attachment and Loss.* New York: Basic Books.

Brown, Tim. 2009. *Change by Design: How Design Thinking Transforms Organizations and Inspires Innovation.* New York: HarperCollins Publishers.

Cavallini, Ilaria, Tiziana Filippini, Vea Vecchi, and Lorella Trancossi. 2011. *The Wonder of Learning: The Hundred Languages of Children.* Reggio Emilia, Italy: Reggio Children.

Counsell, Shelly, Lawrence Escalada, Rosemary Geiken, Melissa Sander, Jill Uhlenberg, Beth Van Meeteren, Sonia Yoshizawa, and Betty Zan. 2015. *STEM Learning with Young Children: Inquiry Teaching with Ramps and Pathways.* New York: Teachers College Press.

Courage, Mary L., and Mark L. Howe. 2010. "To Watch or Not to Watch: Infants and Toddlers in a Brave New Electronic World." *Developmental Review* 30 (2): 101–15.

Daugherty, Michael K. 2013. "The Prospect of an 'A' in STEM Education." *Journal of STEM Education* 14 (2): 10–14.

DeVries, Rheta, and Christina Sales. 2011. *Ramps & Pathways: A Constructivist Approach to Physics with Young Children.* Washington, DC: NAEYC.

DeVries, Rheta, Betty Zan, Carolyn Hildebrandt, Rebecca Edmiaston, and Christina Sales. 2002. *Developing Constructivist Early Childhood Curriculum: Practical Principles and Activities.* New York: Teachers College Press.

Gandini, Lella. 2012. "History, Ideas, and Basic Principles: An Interview with Loris Malaguzzi." In *The Hundred Languages of Children: The Reggio Emilia Experience in Transformation,* edited by Carolyn Edwards, Lella Gandini, and George Forman, 27–73. Santa Barbara, CA: Praeger.

Gopnik, Alison. 2009. *The Philosophical Baby: What Children's Minds Tell Us about Truth, Love, and the Meaning of Life.* New York: Farrar, Strauss and Giroux.

———. 2012. "Scientific Thinking in Young Children: Theoretical Advances, Empirical Research, and Policy Implications." *Science* 337 (6102): 1623–27.

Inhelder, Bärbel, and Jean Piaget. 1958. *The Growth of Logical Thinking from Childhood to Adolescence.* New York: Basic Books.

———. 1964. *The Early Growth of Logic in the Child.* New York: W. W. Norton.

Kamii, Constance, and Rheta DeVries. 1993. *Physical Knowledge in Preschool Education: Implications of Piaget's Theory.* New York: Teachers College Press.

Kelley, Tom, and David Kelley. 2013. *Creative Confidence: Unleashing the Creative Potential within Us All.* New York: Crown Business.

Korbin, Jill E. 2011. "*The Cultural Nature of Human Development.* Barbara Rogoff. New York: Oxford University Press. 2003. xiii 448 pp." *Ethos* 39 (1): 1–2.

Lenz-Taguchi, Hillevi. 2010. *Going beyond the Theory/Practice Divide in Early Childhood Education: Introducing an Intra-Active Pedagogy.* London and New York: Routledge.

Lightfoot, Cynthia, Michael Cole, and Sheila R. Cole. 2013. *The Development of Children.* 7th ed. New York: Worth Publishers.

Maguire-Fong, Mary Jane. 2015. *Teaching and Learning with Infants and Toddlers: Where Meaning-Making Begins.* New York: Teachers College Press and Columbia University Press.

Notari-Syverson, Angela, and Faith H. Sadler. 2008. "Math Is for Everyone: Strategies for Supporting Early Mathematical Competencies in Young Children." *Young Exceptional Children* 11 (3): 2–16.

Piaget, Jean. 1952. *The Child's Conception of Number.* New York: W. W. Norton.

———. 1962. *Play, Dreams and Imitation in Childhood.* New York: W. W. Norton.

———. 1969. *The Construction of Reality in the Child.* New York: Basic Books.

Piaget, Jean, and Bärbel Inhelder. 1967. *The Child's Conception of Space.* New York: W. W. Norton.

———. 1974. *The Child's Construction of Quantities: Conservation and Atomism.* London: Routledge and Kegan Paul.

Piaget, Jean, Bärbel Inhelder, and Alina Szeminska. 1960. *The Child's Conception of Geometry.* New York: W. W. Norton.

Reggio Children. 2011. *I Tempi del Tempo: The Times of Time.* DVD. Reggio Emilia, Italy: Reggio Children.

Rogoff, Barbara. 2003. *The Cultural Nature of Human Development.* Oxford and New York: Oxford University Press.

Vygotsky, Lev S. 1978. *Mind in Society: The Development of Higher Psychological Processes.* Cambridge: Harvard University Press.

Index

mixed-age experiences, 83–84
modeling
    and clay, 14–15, 16, 18
    and material guidelines, 123
    and multipurpose materials, 41
    and paint media example, 141
    and tinkering, 115
motion, 58. *See also* movement
motivation
    and clay, 13, 18
    and environment, 97
    and infant/toddler learning
        approaches, 3
motor development. *See* physical
    development
movement, 57–62
    extension activities, 71
    and music, 64–68
    new experiences, 58–62
multipurpose materials, 39–55
    and environment, 44, 104, 120
    extension activities, 44–45, 55
    and learning scripts, 111–112
    opening and closing, 40–45
    physical properties, 42, 45–47
    and sound, 64
    space and quantity, 48–54
music
    and engineering, 62–64
    extension activities, 71
    and movement, 64–68
    and routines/rituals, 32–35

naming, and sound, 62
naturally occurring opportunities, 10–11
    and community context, 92, 93
    and material guidelines, 123–124
    and routines/rituals, 36–37
    and schedules, 103–104
    See also routines/rituals
Notari-Syverson, Angela, xviii
numeracy
    and multipurpose materials, 49
    and routines/rituals, 31, 34
    See also mathematics

object permanence, 4, 10
observation
    and circuitry, 76, 77, 78
    and clay, 16
    and environment, 100, 101
    and light, 81, 82, 84
    and movement, 61
    and multipurpose materials, 39
    and preschool children, 151–152
obstacles, 131–132
open-ended materials. *See* multipurpose
    materials
open exploration. *See* experiential
    learning
opening and closing, 40–45
opportunities for learning. *See* naturally
    occurring opportunities

paint media example, 137–144
    craft development, 142–143
    design, 143–144
    experiential learning, 140, 141
    family involvement, 142, 144
    learning scripts, 142
    technology, 141–142
    visual displays, 138–140
parallel play, 17
parts-to-whole concept, 16, 31
patterns, 68
pedagogy
    and environment, 95–96
    examples, 1–2
physical development, 1–2, 4
    and movement, 57
    and multipurpose materials, 43
physical knowledge, 8, 9, 58
physical learning space, 101–103, 116
    paint media example, 137, 144
physical properties
    clay, 16
    light, 76, 78, 79, 80
    and multipurpose materials, 42, 45–47
    paint media example, 142
Piaget, Jean
    on classification, 11